THE QUICK
AFTER-WORK
LOW-FAT
COOKBOOK

THE QUICK AFTER-WORK LOW-FAT COOKBOOK

SUE KREITZMAN

PIATKUS

For Katie

First published in 1997 by
Judy Piatkus (Publishers) Ltd
5 Windmill Street, London W1P 1HF

Paperback edition published 1998

The moral right of the author has been asserted
*A catalogue record for this book is available from
the British Library*

ISBN 0-7499-1707-5 hbk
ISBN 0-7499-1806-3 pbk

Designed by Paul Saunders
Illustrations by Madeleine David
Photographs by Steve Baxter
Home economy by Meg Jansz
Styling by Marian Price

Cover design by Jerry Goldie Graphic Design

Front cover photograph by Steve Baxter shows Goat's Cheese
Salad with Golden Spice Pan-Roasted Potatoes and Artichoke
and Cranberry Relish. Back cover photograph shows Grilled
Duck Breast with Sour-Cherry Red-Onion Chutney, Potato
Cakes and Pan-Braised Carrots

Back cover photograph courtesy *Cambridge Evening News*

Typeset by Phoenix Photosetting, Lordswood, Chatham, Kent
Printed and bound in Great Britain by
Mackays of Chatham PLC, Chatham, Kent

Contents

Acknowledgements

HEARTFELT thanks to Sandie Mitchel-King for enabling me to continue a full schedule of cooking, writing and demonstrating, and to Brenda Huebler for keeping chaos at bay.

Exuberant and affectionate salutations to the Roman Road Gang - Katie Ashley and Peter King, Keith Brewster and Peter Nevis, and Shawm Kreitzman - for good food, shared laughter, and a terrific sense of community camaraderie.

Grateful thanks to Janet Tod for adding even more colour to my life and to Graham Douglas for explaining all about Quarks.

Hugs and kisses to Marlena Spieler and Alan McLaughlan for their generous help, support and hospitality, and to Jeanette Hoare and Googie Woodham who add to the quality of life on the Roman.

As always, many happy thank yous to Mandy Morton for our ongoing radio food chats, to David Grossman, agent extraordinaire, who has the most infectious laugh in the known universe, to the Garden Team at the Prospects Trust for cultivating my ineffably fragrant and glorious herb garden and for understanding and indulging my rather odd ideas about colour, to Terry Fisher for keeping the chocolate river flowing, and to my editor, Heather Rocklin: thanks for being *you!*

To my husband Steve, loving thanks for all you have done. I never forget it, and I never take it for granted.

Finally much neighbourly love to the smiling faces up and down the Roman Road: you all make everyday life a great pleasure.

Introduction

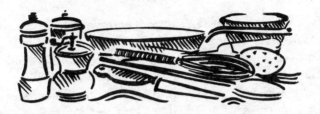

FOOD is one of life's most pleasurable, on-going, sensual adventures. A low-fat, high-nutrition lifestyle doesn't mean that the adventure is over; in fact just the opposite is true – a low-fat regime (once the simple basic techniques of successful low-fat cookery are mastered) is a heightened adventure. Suddenly food tastes fresh, new, clean and vibrant; the palate, freed of blunting, cloying fattiness, revels in new-found glory. Gradually, one slims down and becomes lithe, energetic and nutritionally fulfilled. A switch from a high-fat to a low-fat lifestyle is exhilarating and satisfying – those who feel that it is a life sentence of gastronomic boredom just don't understand!

Fortunately, producing good low-fat meals doesn't demand a major investment of time – in fact it can be joyously slap-dash and immediate. I've put together a collection of quick, no-fuss, colourful and easy-going recipes that take from ten minutes to half an hour to prepare. I must stress that this book is far more about *ideas* than it is about recipes. Once you get the hang of it, you will be able to adapt the techniques and tips to your own culinary ends. All of these recipes are very flexible and forgiving: you can change the seasonings to your taste and fiddle about with the ingredients according to availability, the time of year, your mood and the occasion. I have no interest whatsoever in what's 'in', what's 'out', what fad might possibly strike next year, or what the trendy foodies are praising or sneering at right now. My interest is in low-fat, high-nutrition, good-tasting food that is fun, fast and easy to put together. There is no greater pleasure than standing in a well-stocked kitchen at the end of a long day, waiting for inspiration to strike, then, when it does, throwing together a stunning, impromptu, lightening-quick meal. Enjoy the adventure!

A Note on Timing

All the cooking times suggested in the recipes are *approximate*: standing over the cooker with a stopwatch is *not* a relaxing way to cook! All cooking equipment and ingredients differ, so take the timings as a guide only.

EQUIPMENT

For low-fat cookery (just as for any cookery), you need the usual things: a good set of knives, chopping boards, measuring utensils, wooden spoons, an accurate set of scales, ovenproof glass or Pyroceram baking dishes, spatulas, flexible palette knives, fish slices, a citrus zester, a four-sided grater, whisks, a colander, a nylon sieve, and so on. A blender and food processor are good time-saving investments for puréeing soups and making dips, spreads and pâtés (you can even use the processor for making ice cream, see page 123). Kitchen scissors save valuable time as well – I use them for everything, from snipping herbs and sundried tomatoes to cutting up poultry. A swivel-bladed vegetable peeler will quickly peel raw peppers (see page 9), and a thin metal cake tester is useful for general piercing, as well as for testing cakes.

POTS AND PANS

Heavy-bottomed non-reactive (i.e. will not react with acid ingredients to produce 'off' tastes and colours) pots and pans are best for low-fat cookery: both non-stick and enamelled cast-iron are excellent choices. Attractive pans that can be used on the hob, and then as serving dishes, save time and washing-up. In addition to frying pans and saucepans, a large flat-bottomed non-stick wok with a cover will come in very handy, and not just for stir-frying; it can serve as a saucepan and a steamer (along with a bamboo steamer basket or one of those folding perforated petal jobs) as well. Like a frying pan, a wok gives you more surface area, so that a sauce, a sauté or even a soup will cook faster than it would in a saucepan. A truly wonderful pan to have is a non-stick 'contact grill' pan (the kind that has ridges) that is used on the hob. With no oil at all, or a mere 'spritz' of the oil–water spray (see page 8), you can use it to achieve an indoor barbecue effect – smoky flavour, char-grill marks and all.

   If any of your pots and pans get burnt-on encrustations, don't waste time scrubbing them. Soak them overnight in a slurry of biological detergent and water, then, next day, just rinse clean.

INGREDIENTS

To cook quickly, be prepared: a well-stocked cupboard, freezer and fridge mean that you can waltz into the kitchen at the nth hour to blithely fling together a carefree yet delicious meal. Well, that's the idea anyway. Keep an inspiring and useful collection of cans, bottles, packets and staples on hand and you should be able to cobble together something satisfying without too much effort, and without mounting a major shopping expedition first. At the end of a fraught day, what you most need is the comfort of delicious, nutritious, fulfilling food. Good organisation means that you don't have to descend to the level of unsatisfying and high-fat packet foods and fast foods. The following lists should help you stock up for quick low-fat cookery.

THE STORE-CUPBOARD

Flavouring Ingredients

Assorted mustards: invaluable in vinaigrettes, cooked sauces, dips and spreads. Try to keep Dijon mustard and a milder dark mustard on hand at all times, along with Provençale mustard with garlic and red peppers (now available in several supermarkets).

Sambal oelek: a fiery red Indonesian chilli paste. Even a small amount adds an explosive element to a dish, so use sparingly.

Chinese-style chilli sauce: not as fierce as *sambal oelek*, but satisfyingly piquant.

Black bean sauce: the Chinese kind, now available in most supermarkets. A small amount gives a rich, salty edge to various dishes.

Hoisin sauce: 'Chinese barbecue sauce' is how this thick, complex sweet/musty sauce is often described. It is very good as a component of a stir-fry sauce or smeared on to a steamed Chinese pancake (or even a Mexican tortilla: gastronomically speaking, no one is ethnically pure these days!) which is then used to enwrap grilled meat and vegetables.

Mexican-style salsa: easily made (see page 18) but available in jars and little tubs as well. Look for salsa that contains no modified starch, or it will not taste fresh and authentic.

Tabasco and Worcestershire sauces: I list these together because I invariably use them together, and consider them almost as essential as salt and pepper. Keep them right next to the cooker, to dash into soups and sauces – they are a wonderful shortcut to building deep flavour. (Because Worcestershire sauce contains anchovies, it is not suitable for vegetarians.)

Teriyaki sauce: another essential to keep next to the cooker, for dashing into things when you want to enhance flavour. It is, basically, a flavoured soy sauce. Low-fat mushroom cookery wouldn't be the same without it.

Thai fish sauce: now available in most major supermarkets (how sophisticated we are becoming!), this sauce seems rather smelly, but don't panic; small amounts (a teaspoon or less) give excellent results in all sorts of Thai-inspired dishes. A bottle will last for quite a while.

Ketchup: a tablespoon or so of this old stand-by is great in dipping sauces, spreads and dressings. It is a bright, dependable and homely presence on anyone's store-cupboard shelf.

Balsamic vinegar: great stuff, even the supermarket bottles – not quite the real thing, but delicious, none the less. It does wonders for low-fat salad dressings (see pages 23–7). Stock *cider vinegar, sherry vinegar* and *white wine vinegar* as well.

Mango chutney: I particularly like hot mango chutney, and use it in dressings, sauces and marinades. Buy the best you can find.

Honey: not only useful in dessert cookery, but wonderful in marinades, sauces, dressings – all the usual places where you want to build complex and pleasing flavour in a hurry. It blends beautifully with mustard and with the Chinese condiments.

Spices: buy spices in small jars or cartons and store them *near* the cooker for convenience (not on shelves *over* the cooker or they will turn stale very quickly). The spices called for regularly in this collection are:

ground cayenne
crushed dried chilli flakes
mild chilli powder
ground coriander
ground cumin
various good-quality curry powders
fennel seeds
ground ginger
whole nutmeg
ground Hungarian paprika
ground white pepper
salt and pepper (keep sea salt and whole black peppercorns in grinders next to the cooker)
sesame seeds
tandoori spice mix

Canned and Bottled Goods

Vegetable bouillon powder

Red peppers (sometimes called pimentos): in brine: don't buy the ones in vinegar or oil)

Artichoke hearts: in brine

Corn kernels (extra sweet)

Tuna fish: in brine or spring water

Smoked tuna fish

Red salmon

Black olives: bottled in brine or vacuum-packed

Capers

Canned beans and pulses:

black-eyed beans	butter beans
borlotti beans	chick peas
cannellini beans	lentils
red kidney beans	

Dried Goods

Tiny red lentils: the only readily available fast-cooking dried pulse

Assorted dried fruit: apricots, cherries, blueberries, cranberries, figs, raisins, sultanas

Tomato Products

Sundried tomatoes: how did we live without them? Snip them into fine dice with scissors, and use as part of a flavour infusion (see pages 7–10). Buy them dry-packed, not swimming in oil. They add a compelling, smoky, caramelised dimension to all sorts of savoury dishes. Some are salty, so be careful about adding additional salt. There is no need to reconstitute them first – they rehydrate as they cook.

Canned tomatoes: whole and chopped

Passata: in cartons

Tomato paste (purée): in tubes (you will only be using a small amount at a time)

THE FREEZER

Prawns

Various stocks: fish, vegetable, chicken (see page 8)

Fruit: blueberries and raspberries

Frozen vegetables: corn and peas freeze very well. Others lose texture, but this doesn't matter if they are to be used in puréed soups. Frozen vegetables are usually frozen very quickly indeed after harvesting, so may actually be 'fresher' than supermarket green-grocery department produce that travels the world to reach our local supermarkets.

Microwave rice: Try to find the kind packed in individual sachets.

THE FRIDGE

Skimmed milk

Very low fat fromage frais

Quark: lovely smooth and creamy no-fat curd cheese; a basic ingredient in many spreads and dips

Medium-fat Italian-style mozzarella cheese: in liquid-filled pouches, and only 10 per cent fat. If you can't find it, use the ordinary Italian-style mozzarella (also in liquid-filled pouches) – only 15 per cent fat.

Ricotta cheese: at 15 per cent fat, this is a wonderful stand-in for crème fraîche and mascarpone cheese – both 80 per cent fat! It is no compromise; ricotta is sweet, fresh-tasting and delicious, rich yet not at all cloying.

Parmesan cheese: in a piece – grate it as you need it. Parmesan is a medium-fat cheese with a deep and wonderful taste – a little goes a long way.

Boursin Léger: low-fat garlic and herb cheese spread

Free-range eggs: the yolks are high in fat and cholesterol, but the whites (very useful in all sorts of ways) are fat-free.

Baguette dough: in tubes

Fresh herbs

Spring onions

MISCELLANEOUS

Citrus fruits: lemons, limes, oranges

Flavour vegetables: onions (red and yellow); chillies (the smaller they are, the hotter they are); garlic (don't store in the fridge, or the bulbs will sprout); ginger root

Beetroot: natural, vacuum-packed (no vinegar)

Breadcrumbs: plain, uncoloured and unseasoned (save dry bread to make your own)

Mexican tortillas: wheat and maize

Chinese pancakes

Carbohydrate Basics

Potatoes

Quick-cooking polenta

Couscous

Bulghur

Assorted dried pasta, including Chinese noodles

Fresh lasagne sheets: refrigerate

Potato gnocchi (see page 52)

Instant potato flakes: such as Mr Mash or Waitrose own brand

Wines and Spirits

Wine and vermouth: give untold depths to low-fat food – rapid cooking evaporates the alcohol, so you are left with gorgeous flavour, but no inebriating, fattening alcohol calories.

Dry red and dry white wine

Medium dry sherry

THE BASICS

You will use these few techniques and tips over and over again, as you get to know your way around the low-fat kitchen. The stock sauté and oil–water spray will change your life – substituting them for the usual oceans of oil, butter or margarine will save you many thousands of fat calories each week. The lack of those oceans will unleash flavour and texture in a most remarkable way.

STOCK SAUTÉ

A true low-fat diet means no oil, butter, margarine, lard, chicken fat or dripping, but without these, how can you make the basic vegetable sauté that begins so many savoury recipes? It's quite simple, use stock (vegetable, fish or chicken, depending on the recipe) or, even better, stock and wine, as the sauté base. Good unseasoned stock is now available in little tubs in many supermarkets. Freeze the little tubs, thaw them when needed in the microwave or under running hot water, then dilute the stock with water to 2–3 times its volume.

Another stock option is to use good vegetable bouillon powder (Marigold brand is excellent -- especially the vegan powder which is low in salt). Stock cubes tend to be much too salty, chemical-tasting and surprisingly high in fat. To use the powder, simply put the flavour vegetables in the pan with water (and wine if you wish) and sprinkle in a couple of pinches of the powder. Add some slivered black olives to add an olive oil dimension with just a fraction of the fat of the actual oil. (Canned, stoned black olives are flabby and tasteless; seek out olives on the stone, bottled in brine, or vacuum-packed.)

A typical sauté base for a sauce or a soup might contain, along with the stock and wine, snipped sundried tomatoes, slivered black olives, crushed garlic, diced onions and a pinch of crushed dried chillies. This forms an infusion that helps to imbue the dish with real depth of flavour. Vegetable stock (the liquid or the excellent powder) makes a good all-purpose stock which can be used wherever stock is called for in this book. Chicken and vegetable stocks are interchangeable. Use fish stock for fish recipes, but, if you have none, substitute vegetable or chicken stock.

OIL–WATER SPRAY

Oil is simply liquid fat, which is why I use the stock-sauté method, and avoid oil almost entirely. The exception is this spray. It delivers a fine mist of oil and water (the amount of oil is minuscule) that nicely greases a pan or lubricates ingredients to be grilled. Buy a new plastic perfume spray atomiser or a small plant mister, clean it thoroughly, and fill it seven-eighths full with water and one-eighth with oil. I keep three sprays going at all times: one filled with olive oil, another with safflower oil and a third with sesame oil. To use, shake and spray.

PEPPERS

Peppers in all their multi-coloured glory are extraordinarily useful to a low-fat cook. Their flavour, texture and digestibility are greatly improved if they are peeled first.

To Peel a Pepper by Char-Grilling

This produces tender, supple, ineffably sweet cooked pepper flesh that is exquisite as it is – even more so puréed into a silken sauce.

1. If you have a gas hob, char the whole pepper directly on the gas flame, turning it with tongs as the skin blackens and blisters. Otherwise, cut it in half, remove the core, seeds and ribs, bend it so that it 'breaks' slightly and will lie flat, and place, skin up, under a hot grill until the skin chars.

2. Put the blackened pepper in a bowl, cover with a plate or cling film, and leave for 3–5 minutes (longer if necessary), then carefully (it's hot!) slip off and discard the blackened skin. Don't rinse the pepper or it will lose some of its compelling smokiness. Be sure to save the delicious accumulated juices to use with the pepper.

To Peel a Raw Pepper

It may seem like unnecessary fiddling to peel raw peppers, but believe me, it is worth the few seconds of extra work. Although pepper flesh is sweet and crisp, the skin is tough, indigestible and sometimes slightly bitter. And when unskinned raw peppers are sautéed or stir-fried, the skins roll up into unpleasant little sticks that ruin the finished dish.

1. Halve the raw pepper and remove the core, seeds and ribs.

2. Cut the pepper into its natural sections and peel with a swivel-bladed vegetable peeler.

GARLIC

Roasting whole garlic bulbs for an hour in a hot oven results in a deeply flavoured (yet surprisingly mellow) purée that can be used to enrich many low-fat dishes. For a faster method (but just as satisfying), pan-braise garlic cloves in stock. The purée is infinitely useful, even if just whipped with quark or fromage frais and then spread on toast, dolloped into a jacket potato or folded into freshly cooked pasta shapes (add some chopped herbs and grated Parmesan to make it perfect). When used in sauces, spreads and so on, the purée adds a gently aromatic garlic presence that is quite different from the harsh rudeness of raw garlic.

To Pan-Braise Garlic

Peel any number of garlic cloves, but don't crush them. Spread them in a heavy-bottomed frying pan and cover generously with stock. Cover tightly, and simmer for 10–15 minutes, until the garlic is meltingly tender and the stock greatly reduced (check and top up the stock if necessary as the cloves braise). Drain, saving any left-over stock for soups and sauces. To purée, mash the cloves or push them through a fine nylon sieve.

TOMATOES

I am a tomato fanatic. The vine tomatoes and 'flavour' tomatoes available now in supermarkets fill me with delight, but to make the most of them, you must plan ahead. To be at their best, they must ripen for a few days at room temperature, so buy them, bring them home, slit the package open so that they can breathe, and let them sit on the counter for a few days, until they are still firm but bursting with juice and flavour. Don't refrigerate them, or the flavour will never develop. Cherry tomatoes tend to have plenty of real tomato taste as well, but the same rules apply.

To Peel and Deseed a Tomato

Blanch the tomato in boiling water for 10 seconds. (For speed, boil the water in the kettle, then pour it over the tomatoes in a bowl.) Refresh under cold water, then cut out the cores, and slip off the skins. Halve the tomatoes and use your fingers to ease out the seeds.

MANGOES

Mangoes are almost indecently luscious (juicy, sloppy, sweet, indulgent: all of that and more), and they are now available in quantity all year round. No wonder many of us throw them into everything we possibly can.

To Peel and Dice a Mango

1. With a sharp knife, cut straight down the length of the mango, cutting off one 'cheek' but missing the large flat centre stone. Repeat on the other side, with the second 'cheek'.

2. With a small paring knife, score each mango in half lengthways and crossways, cutting through the flesh all the way to, but not through, the skin. Push out the skin as if you were pushing the mango half inside out. The mango flesh will stand out in cubes. Slice these cubes off the skin.

3. Peel the skin from the centre slice left on the stone, and – as best you can – slice the mango flesh off the stone. Do this over a bowl to save losing any of the juices.

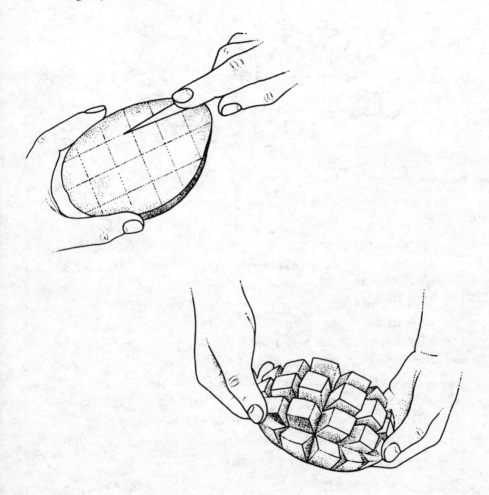

· CHAPTER 1 ·

Embellishments

FAST meals are often simple meals: a poached fish fillet, a sautéed chicken breast, a grilled chop – quick and easy, but no pizzazz whatsoever. A treasure trove of recipes follows, meant to add a bit of excitement to the simple things: a few spoonfuls of chilli-laced salsa to nestle next to a perfectly cooked fish fillet; a vivid purée of beetroot or grilled pepper to swirl on to the surface of a bowl of smooth soup; a crisp fresh vegetable relish to dollop on to a juicy burger. All of these are quickly made, and add colour and glamour to fast food. Many are multi-purpose: some of the swirls can be used as sauces and dips; some of the salsas and relishes can be served as salads; the dips and spreads can be served as starters with crudités and toast; and several of the dressings also double as marinades and basting sauces.

DIPS AND SPREADS

Beetroot Purée

MAKES ½ PINT (300 ml)

FOR this red-blooded dip or spread, use vacuum-packed natural (no vinegar) cooked beetroot. Try beetroot purée as a sandwich spread, a filling for little mushroom caps, chicory leaves and pepper boats, or just spread on toast or savoury biscuits for a colourful snack. And beetroot purée is incomparable dolloped icy cold, on to piping hot, freshly steamed new potatoes that have been roughly broken open with a fork. For a change, make an even simpler beetroot purée by puréeing the cooked beetroot with 1–2 tablespoons of your favourite no-fat chutney.

————— • —————

9 oz (250 g) vacuum-packed cooked
  beetroot (no vinegar)
1 tablespoon very low fat fromage frais
½ tablespoon balsamic vinegar

pan-braised garlic (see page 10), to taste
  (an entire head would not be amiss)
salt and freshly ground pepper, to taste

————— • —————

1. Cut the beetroot into chunks and put in a food processor or blender with the remaining ingredients. Process to a rough purée.

2. Scrape into a bowl, cover and store in the fridge.

Herbed Goat's Cheese Raita

MAKES 6 fl oz (175 ml)

LITTLE pots of creamy goat's cheese (they weigh in at about ten per cent fat) are a welcome addition to supermarket dairy cabinets. Lighten the cheese with low-fat fromage frais flavoured with fresh herbs, and use it as a garnish for vegetable stews, or spread it on hot toast.

——— ▪ ———

4–5 oz (125 g) pot of medium-fat goat's cheese

2–3 tablespoons chopped fresh mixed

herbs (e.g chives, basil and flat-leaf parsley)

2 tablespoons very low fat fromage frais

——— ▪ ———

Put all the ingredients in a food processor, and process until well combined.

Smoked Trout Pâté

MAKES 8 fl oz (225 ml)

TO MAKE the simplest smoked fish pâté imaginable, just blend together some smoked fish, some quark (or fromage frais) and a scattering of fresh herbs. If you are feeling flush, try smoked salmon instead of trout, and spread it thickly on a toasted bagel.

——— ▪ ———

6–8 oz (175–225 g) smoked trout fillets, flaked

7 oz (200 g) carton quark, or use very low fat fromage frais

2 tablespoons chopped fresh chives

1 tablespoon chopped fresh parsley

a few drops of lime juice

several dashes of Tabasco sauce

freshly ground pepper, to taste

——— ▪ ———

Combine all the ingredients in a food processor, and process until smooth and creamy.

SWIRLS FOR SOUPS AND STEWS

Swirls are charming soup adornments. A basic vegetable purée soup (see soup chapter for specific recipes) with a vividly colour-contrasted swirl spiralled on to its surface is stunning. Just because food is quickly cooked doesn't mean it shouldn't be intensely pleasurable to *all* the senses. Make it as beautiful as possible and eat it with great pleasure.

A spoonful of salsa, relish or chutney (see pages 18–22) can be tenderly placed in the centre of the swirl, carefully balanced on the surface of the soup. It's not only the look of it that is so enchanting; the combination of tastes and textures makes a simple bowlful of soup a mosaic of colour, taste and texture.

Chilli Swirl or Sauce

MAKES ½ PINT (300 ml)

NOT just a swirl but a splendid sauce or dip as well. If you can't find bottled or canned peppers, grilled fresh peppers are easy to prepare (see page 9). You will need about four large peppers. If you can't find *sambal oelek* (although it *is* available in many supermarkets), use chilli sauce instead. Increase the amount of *sambal oelek* at your own peril!

———— ▪ ————

15 oz (425 g) jar or can red peppers, drained, or 4 char-grilled peppers (see page 9), peeled and roughly chopped

1 teaspoon sambal oelek (*Indonesian hot chilli paste*)
½ teaspoon runny honey

———— ▪ ————

Combine the ingredients in a blender, and purée until smooth.

Pepper Swirl or Spread

MAKES ½ PINT (300 ml)

A CREAMY and mild swirl (well, milder than Chilli Swirl at any rate) to adorn a colour-contrasted soup, or to spread in a sandwich.

———— ▪ ————

2 canned peppers, drained, or 2 char-
   grilled peppers (see page 9), peeled
   and roughly chopped
1 rounded teaspoon Dijon mustard

1 rounded tablespoon fromage frais
2–3 dashes of Tabasco sauce
2–3 dashes of Worcestershire sauce

———— ▪ ————

Combine the ingredients in a blender, and purée until smooth.

White Bean Swirl or Dip

MAKES ½ PINT (300 ml)

D OUBLE the quantities for this recipe, thin with stock and you will have a velvety smooth and subtle soup. For vivid contrast, top with Chilli Swirl (see page 15). Otherwise, follow the recipe as it is, and swirl it on top of Curried Pea Soup (see page 35) or Spinach Soup (see page 38).

———— ▪ ————

14 oz (400 g) can of cannellini beans,
   drained and rinsed
juice of ½ orange
several dashes of Tabasco sauce
several dashes of teriyaki sauce

1 tablespoon tomato purée
1 teaspoon mild korma curry powder
½ teaspoon runny honey
1 tablespoon medium dry sherry
4–6 tablespoons vegetable stock

———— ▪ ————

Combine all the ingredients in a blender, and purée until very smooth.

Beetroot Swirl

MAKES ½ PINT (300 ml)

B ANISH all thoughts of watery, acrid beetroot. Doused with bad vinegar, it's pathetic, but treated properly it is an earthy and exciting root. This swirl is stunning on a pale green soup.

———— ∎ ————

2 vacuum-packed cooked beetroot (no vinegar)

juice of ½ orange
½ tablespoon hot mango chutney

———— ∎ ————

1. Cut the beetroot into chunks, reserving the juice, and put in a blender with the remaining ingredients.

2. Add the beetroot juice, and purée until perfectly smooth.

Roasted Tomato Swirl

MAKES ½ PINT (300 ml)

A RIDGED 'grill' pan (that you use on the hob), if you have one, gives the tomatoes a smoky, barbecued taste. If you haven't got one, use a heavy-bottomed non-stick frying pan, or sear the tomatoes under the grill or in a gas flame. When you swirl this on to a bowl of soup, top with a scattering of fresh basil shreds.

———— ∎ ————

olive oil–water spray (see page 8)
6 'flavour' tomatoes (approximately 12 oz/350 g)

2 tablespoons tomato purée
several dashes of Tabasco sauce
several dashes of Worcestershire sauce

———— ∎ ————

1. Spray a ridged 'grill' pan with oil–water spray and heat. Sear the tomatoes all over until they are covered in blackened patches. Cool briefly.

2. Pull off the tomato skins, cut out the cores and put the tomatoes in a food processor or blender with the remaining ingredients.

3. Process until smooth, then push through a nylon sieve.

SALSAS, RELISHES AND CHUTNEYS

What is the difference between a salsa and a relish? They are both zesty mixtures of finely chopped raw vegetables, sometimes mixed with fruit, used as a table condiment to liven up a meal. The current rage for chilli-laced salsas originated with the simple table salsas of Mexico, which are part sauce, part relish, and in some ways very like fresh chutneys. These days, all sorts of fanciful concoctions are put together in the name of salsa, many of them, I must say, wonderfully exhilarating, although not particularly traditional. Some of the recipes in this collection seem more relish than salsa, and I have named them accordingly, although it is sometimes hard to pinpoint exactly what led to the decision; perhaps a mixture is more relish than salsa when the chunks of vegetables and fruit are larger. A chutney is a sort of cooked relish, although there are raw chutneys as well. An attempt at proper classification will drive you dizzy, but they all provide a welcome touch of zest to your fast food.

Fresh Tomato Salsa

MAKES ½ PINT (300 ml)

ALTHOUGH the balsamic vinegar is not typical, this recipe is very like the simple table salsas found in parts of Mexico. It won't work unless the tomatoes are very good indeed.

—————— ▪ ——————

½ red onion, diced
1 garlic clove, crushed
½–1 chilli, deseeded and diced
½ tablespoon balsamic vinegar
juice of 1 lime

6 ripe tomatoes, deseeded and roughly
  diced
1–2 tablespoons chopped fresh coriander
1–2 tablespoons chopped fresh parsley

—————— ▪ ——————

1. Combine the onion, garlic and chilli with the vinegar and lime juice, and leave to marinate for a few minutes.

2. Add the tomatoes and fresh herbs, and mix to combine.

Simple Tomato Salsa

MAKES 1½ PINTS (900 ml)

THIS is a very simple and basic salsa, not unlike what you might find served with tortilla chips at a Mexican restaurant. It is *very* good. If fresh, flavourful tomatoes are available, peel, deseed and dice a few and stir them in. I sometimes substitute shredded basil for the coriander, and add some slivered black olives and a few diced grilled peppers and their juices. With these simple additions, I have been known to serve it in bowls and call it 'Chunky Gazpacho'.

---

2 garlic cloves, crushed
1–2 chillies, deseeded and diced
2 tablespoons balsamic vinegar
2 tablespoons good red wine vinegar
two 14 oz (400 g) cans chopped
  tomatoes

2–3 tablespoons chopped fresh coriander
2–3 tablespoons chopped fresh parsley
2 spring onions, trimmed and thinly
  sliced
salt, to taste (if needed)

---

1. Combine the garlic, chillies and vinegar in a small jug or bowl and leave to marinate for 5–10 minutes.

2. Combine with all the remaining ingredients, adding salt to taste, if needed.

Peach Salsa

MAKES ½ PINT (300 ml)

I LOVE this nestled on top of a serving of soup, in the centre of a swirl. Try it on Red Lentil–Vegetable Soup (see page 32). I tried this recipe once with canned peaches and, although it lacked the incomparable fresh and fragrant succulence of the fresh version, it wasn't half bad.

———— • ————

2 fresh peaches, stoned and diced
1 tablespoon chopped fresh coriander
1 tablespoon chopped fresh mint
1 small red onion, finely diced

juice of 1 lime
1½ teaspoons balsamic vinegar
½ chilli, deseeded and diced

———— • ————

Combine all the ingredients in a bowl.

Artichoke and Cranberry Relish

MAKES 1½ PINTS (900 ml)

S ERVE these balsamic- and vermouth-bathed artichoke hearts and cranberries as a relish with meat, fish or poultry, or serve spooned into pita pockets with one of the creamy dressings (see pages 26–7). It makes a dandy snack, too, for those with a 'savoury tooth', who find themselves browsing disconsolately through the fridge in search of a little something.

———— • ————

6 oz (175 g) dried cranberries
8 fl oz (225 ml) dry white vermouth
two 14 oz (400 g) cans artichoke hearts
   in brine, drained and quartered

juice of 1 large lemon
2 tablespoons balsamic or sherry vinegar
freshly ground pepper, to taste

———— • ————

1. Put the cranberries and vermouth in a frying pan, and simmer for about 10 minutes, until the liquid is absorbed and the cranberries are plump.

2. Toss in a bowl with the remaining ingredients.

3. Serve at room temperature.

Olive and Cherry Tomato Relish

MAKES 2 PINTS (1.1 litres)

FOR AN easy-to-prepare relish that overflows with real tomato flavour, try cherry tomatoes. Buy them a few days before you plan to use them, and let them sit in a cool part of the kitchen until they are needed. For the simplest tomato relish imaginable, quarter as many cherry tomatoes as you like, salt lightly, toss with a handful of shredded fresh basil leaves, and drizzle with balsamic vinegar. Leave to sit for about 30 minutes. If the tomatoes are good, it never fails to light up the eyes of those who taste it for the first time. The following relish is a light, tomato-augmented version of traditional Italian olive salad. Lavish it generously on to sandwiches of sliced lean Italian meats and grilled peppers, spoon it on to burgers (see pages 92–3) or serve as a salad accompaniment.

---

18 oz (500 g) firm, ripe cherry tomatoes, stemmed and quartered (use half red, half yellow cherry tomatoes, if they are available)

5 green olives in brine, drained and sliced off the stones into slivers

5 black olives in brine, drained and sliced off the stones into slivers

2 teaspoons brine from olive jar

1 chilli, deseeded and finely chopped

1½ tablespoons drained capers

1½ tablespoons balsamic vinegar

1–3 garlic cloves, crushed (the amount depends on your taste)

juice of ½ lemon

3 spring onions, trimmed and thinly sliced

2 tablespoons chopped fresh parsley (flat-leaf if possible)

2 tablespoons shredded fresh mint or basil

freshly ground pepper, to taste

Combine all the ingredients in a bowl, and let stand at room temperature until serving time, stirring occasionally. (To keep for more than a few hours, store in the refrigerator.)

Fig and Chilli Chutney

MAKES ½ PINT (300 ml)

THIS is quite piquant. Tone it down if you wish by decreasing the chillies and the Tabasco dashes, but don't omit them entirely, or you will miss the fun; figs and chillies are fabulous partners. Fig and Chilli Chutney would do wonders for grilled duck breast, or, for a snack with great character, dollop it on top of a matzo cracker spread with quark or fromage frais. The chutney will keep for at least a week in the fridge.

½ red chilli, deseeded and roughly chopped

½ green chilli, deseeded and roughly chopped

8 ready-to-eat dried figs, stemmed and cut into 6 pieces each

5 dry-pack sundried tomatoes, very roughly chopped (use scissors)

½ inch (1 cm) piece fresh root ginger, peeled and crushed

3–4 garlic cloves, roughly crushed

juice and grated rind of ½ orange

juice and grated rind of ½ lime

diced pulp of ½ orange

1 tablespoon Worcestershire sauce

several dashes of Tabasco sauce

1 tablespoon balsamic vinegar

½ teaspoon paprika

½ teaspoon ground cumin

½ pint (300 ml) vegetable stock

1 tablespoon fresh chopped coriander

1 tablespoon chopped fresh parsley

---

1. Put all the ingredients, except the fresh herbs, in a frying pan, and simmer for approximately 10 minutes, until thickened and syrupy.

2. Stir in the herbs and leave to cool. Transfer to a clean bowl and store in the fridge.

VINAIGRETTES

Alas, for ardent followers of a low-fat lifestyle, dressing a salad properly is a perennial problem. I've been working on this for years; my goal has been to produce a really good no-fat vinaigrette. Of course 'no-fat' means no olive oil (oils are simply liquid fat), and no olive oil means, essentially, no vinaigrette, since vinaigrette is, by definition, a blend of oil, vinegar, mustard (usually) and seasonings. But I'm bending the rules, and calling my new batch of no-oil dressings 'vinaigrettes' – they are astoundingly good.

The alternative vinaigrette base I suggest is a mixture of citrus juices, teriyaki, Tabasco and Worcestershire sauces, balsamic vinegar, crushed garlic, and a pinch of sugar to balance the acidity. Into this basic mix is blended Dijon mustard, and an extra ingredient (you will have several choices) designed (along with the mustard) to add body, and increase the 'cling' factor. The resulting dressing will lightly coat the greens, but will never be sludgy or slimy, as so many of the gum-and-modified-starch-filled no-fat commercial dressings can be.

Not only do these 'vinaigrettes' serve as salad dressings; they can also be used as marinades and basting sauces for quick-cooking pieces of meat, fish and poultry. Because the vinaigrette base will last for weeks in the fridge, it pays to have several jarfuls on hand so that you can quickly add the final thickening ingredients at the last moment, according to the nature of the meal. Once blended, the complete vinaigrette will keep in the fridge for at least two weeks.

Vinaigrette Base

MAKES ½ PINT (300 ml)

—————— • ——————

3 fl oz (75 ml) balsamic vinegar
3 fl oz (75 ml) lime juice or lemon juice
  (or a combination)
3 fl oz (75 ml) orange juice
2 teaspoons teriyaki sauce

several dashes of Tabasco sauce
several dashes of Worcestershire sauce
2 garlic cloves, crushed
pinch or two of sugar, to taste

—————— • ——————

Put all the ingredients in a screw-top jar, put on the lid and shake well.

Red Pepper Mustard Vinaigrette

MAKES ½ PINT (300 ml)

THIS is my star vinaigrette. The pepper gives it a smoky silkiness that exquisitely sets off greens (especially peppery ones). It's worth searching for Provençale mustard flavoured with garlic and red peppers (made by Maille, many supermarkets stock it) but Dijon will do, as will a canned pepper if you don't feel like grilling one. The colour, by the way – a glowing terracotta – is magnificent.

— ▪ —

½ pint (300 ml) Vinaigrette Base (see page 23)

½ char-grilled pepper (see page 9), peeled or ½ canned or bottled pepper, drained

2 tablespoons Provençale mustard with garlic and red peppers or Dijon mustard

— ▪ —

Put all the ingredients in a blender, and purée until smooth.

White Bean and Olive Vinaigrette

MAKES ½ PINT (300 ml)

THE white beans add a smooth, sensual texture; the black olives add an olive oil aroma. Use the rest of the white beans in White Bean Swirl (see page 16) or Bean Chilli (see page 104) in place of one of the cans of borlotti beans.

— ▪ —

½ pint (300 ml) Vinaigrette Base (see page 23)

2 tablespoons canned cannellini beans, drained

2 teaspoons Dijon mustard

3 black olives in brine, drained and slivered off their stones

— ▪ —

Put all the ingredients in a blender, and purée until smooth.

Garlic Vinaigrette

MAKES ½ PINT (300 ml)

Pan-braised garlic, mild yet intense (a perfume rather than a stink) can be added, with great effect, to just about anything. (I occasionally make a perfectly delightful garlic custard – for dessert! But that's another book entirely.)

——— ∎ ———

½ pint (300 ml) Vinaigrette Base (see page 23)
5–6 garlic cloves (or more to taste), pan–braised (see page 10)

2 tablespoons chopped fresh parsley
2 teaspoons Dijon mustard

——— ∎ ———

Put all the ingredients in a blender, and purée until smooth.

Honey and Mustard Vinaigrette

MAKES ½ PINT (300 ml)

A lovely salad dressing for those who like a touch of sweetness with their salad, but this really comes into its own as a marinade, or a basting sauce for chicken pieces or pork tenderloin. Marinate the meat or poultry for as long as you can manage (from ten minutes to overnight), then grill – on a barbecue, under a grill, or in a ridged 'grill' pan that has been oil-and-water sprayed. Brush with the dressing as you turn the pieces.

——— ∎ ———

½ pint (300 ml) Vinaigrette Base without the sugar (see page 23)

2 teaspoons Dijon mustard
1–1½ teaspoons runny honey

——— ∎ ———

Put all the ingredients in a blender, and purée until smooth.

Mango Chutney Vinaigrette

MAKES 12 fl oz (350 ml)

LIKE the Honey and Mustard Vinaigrette, this one makes a heavenly marinade and basting sauce, as well as an excellent salad dressing.

½ pint (300 ml) Vinaigrette Base (see page 23)
½ inch (1 cm) piece fresh root ginger, peeled and crushed

2 teaspoons Dijon mustard
1 tablespoon hot mango chutney

Put all the ingredients in a blender, and purée until smooth.

MAYONNAISE

Vinaigrettes are wonderful but sometimes mayonnaise is just the thing. These creamy dressings (based on no-fat fromage frais) can be used in place of real mayonnaise (pure fat; just thinking about it makes me fatter!).

Fromage Frais 'Mayo'

MAKES ¾ PINT (450 ml)

NOT really a mayonnaise (no egg yolks, no oil) but very useful for those mayonnaise moments. It will keep for several days in the fridge. See page 28 (after the colour plates) for interesting variations.

---

18 oz (500 g) carton very low fat fromage frais
1 tablespoon balsamic vinegar

1 teaspoon Dijon mustard
salt and freshly ground pepper, to taste

Place all the ingredients in a bowl, and whisk well to combine. Refrigerate.

Fromage Frais 'Mayo' Variations

Blend in any of the following (singly or in combinations), according to your taste: Puréed pan-braised garlic (see page 10); Excellent-quality curry powder; *Sambal oelek*; Chopped fresh herbs; Shredded smoked salmon; A dab of tomato purée or ketchup; A tablespoon or so of tomato salsa (see pages 18–19).

Mango and Pepper 'Mayo'

MAKES 12 fl oz (350 ml)

M ANGO, one of the most voluptuous of fruits, and ultra-voluptuous grilled peppers make the best of all creamy dressings. Try it with prawns or as a vivid and luscious sandwich spread – it will transform the simplest sandwich.

———— ▪ ————

1 whole, ripe mango, peeled and cubed (see page 10)
3 tablespoons very low fat fromage frais
dash of Worcestershire sauce
juice of ½–1 lime (to taste)
1 tablespoon Dijon mustard (or Provençale mustard with garlic and red peppers, if available)

1 char-grilled pepper (see page 9), peeled, or 1 canned or bottled pepper, drained
1 tablespoon balsamic vinegar
salt and pepper, to taste

———— ▪ ————

Put all the ingredients in a blender, and purée until perfectly smooth.

PREVIOUS PAGE Red Lentil-Vegetable Soup (page 32) garnished with Beetroot Swirl (page 17) and Peach Salsa (page 20)

OPPOSITE Vegetable Stew (page 108) on couscous (page 53), served with Fig and Chilli Chutney (page 22), Chilli Sauce (page 15) and Herbed Goat's Cheese Raita (page 14)

SAUCES

Ten-Minute Tomato Sauce

MAKES 18 fl oz (500 ml)

A GOOD tomato sauce is one of the most versatile basic recipes in a low-fat cook's repertoire. This one is very satisfying, despite being made in only ten minutes. Use it on pasta, as the topping on a polenta pizza (see page 56), as the base for all sorts of vegetable stews, or with quick-grilled steak for a bracing steak pizzaiola. Passata is simply sieved tomatoes – very smooth and intensely tomatoey, and a welcome addition to the panoply of tomato products available in the supermarket.

———— • ————

5–6 spring onions, trimmed and sliced
2–3 black olives in brine, drained and slivered off their stones
3–4 dry-pack sundried tomatoes, chopped (use scissors)
1–2 garlic cloves, crushed
pinch or two of crushed dried chillies
pinch or two of dried oregano

6–8 fl oz (175–225 ml) stock
18 oz (500 g) carton passata
freshly ground pepper, to taste
1 tablespoon chopped fresh parsley
½ tablespoon chopped fresh basil

———— • ————

1. Combine the onions, olives, sundried tomatoes, garlic, chillies, oregano and stock in a non-reactive frying pan. Cover and boil for 3–4 minutes. Uncover, reduce the heat, and simmer for approximately 10 minutes, until the onions and garlic are tender and the liquid has cooked down considerably and become syrupy.

2. Stir in the passata and grind in some pepper. Simmer for approximately 5 minutes, then stir in the fresh herbs.

Variations

To the basic infusion in step 1 of the above recipe, add one of the following sauces:

Curry Sauce

1 tablespoon good curry powder along with a crushed piece of peeled root ginger.

Mexican Sauce

½ tablespoon each of ground coriander and cumin, along with a pinch of cinnamon and a chopped and deseeded fresh chilli.

Piquant Orange-Scented Sauce

2 tablespoons fresh orange juice, the grated rind of ¼ orange, 1 tablespoon drained capers and ¼ teaspoon chilli sauce.

Rémoulade Sauce

MAKES APPROXIMATELY ¾ PINT (450 ml)

THINK of rémoulade as an elegant tartare sauce, and serve it with crumbed grilled fish, fish cakes or steamed prawns, or use as a sandwich spread.

———— ∎ ————

¾ pint (450 ml) no-fat fromage frais
1 teaspoon Dijon mustard
2 tablespoons drained capers, chopped
2 tablespoons chopped cornichons (small gherkins)

2 tablespoons chopped fresh parsley
½ teaspoon paprika
3 spring onions, trimmed and chopped
several dashes of Tabasco sauce
½ teaspoon dried tarragon, crumbled

———— ∎ ————

Combine all the ingredients in a bowl, cover and refrigerate.

CHAPTER 2

Soups

SOUP-MAKING is particularly satisfying for hurried, slap-dash cooks. Thaw some stock, make a quick flavour infusion, throw in a bit of this and a bit of that, let bubble cheerfully for a few minutes, and *voilà* – a steaming, brimming bowlful of comfort. A few of these soups are made in a wok, that most useful of cookpots, because it deals quickly and efficiently with all the stages of soup-making, from sautéeing the flavour base to simmering. If you don't have a wok, an ordinary saucepan will do, so don't worry too much about it. Several of the soups are puréed in the blender. Because they will still be hot when they go into the blender, it is *very important* to do it in batches; fill the blender goblet only half (or less) full, and hold down the cover. If you overfill the goblet, the hot soup may blow the cover off, surge up and do serious damage, so *be careful*!

Most of these soups are substantial enough to serve as a main course with some good bread. Remember to garnish the soup with a jewel-like cluster of salsa, surrounded by a richly coloured swirl (see pages 15–22) – the garnish changes a nice bowlful of soup into a memorable one.

Some of these soups take 15–20 minutes to prepare; others approximately half an hour. For most of them, part of the cooking time is unattended simmering. While the pot bubbles happily away to itself, rustle up a salad with a fabulous dressing, put out some crusty bread with one of the dips or spreads in chapter 1, or slap together a good sandwich, and you will have an easy and supremely comforting feast.

Red Lentil–Vegetable Soup

MAKES 3½ PINTS (2.1 litres)

RED LENTILS cook quickly with no preliminary soaking. Don't add salt until they are tender, or they will never soften. The lentils, red onions, carrots and peppers combine to make a velvety soup of the most extraordinary glowing copper – breathtaking!

•

5 large carrots, chopped
2 red onions, chopped
5 garlic cloves, chopped
1 tablespoon ground coriander
1 tablespoon ground cumin
½ teaspoon ground turmeric
pinch of ground cayenne, or to taste
several dashes of Tabasco sauce
several dashes of Worcestershire sauce
½ pint (300 ml) unsalted stock
12 oz (350 g) tiny red lentils

3 pints (1.7 litres) unsalted stock, or
    water and vegetable bouillon powder
15 oz (425 g) jar or can red peppers,
    drained, or 3–4 char-grilled peppers,
    peeled (see page 9)
salt and freshly ground pepper, to taste
4 tablespoons chopped fresh coriander

To serve
Peach Salsa (see page 20) or bought hot
    mango chutney
Beetroot Swirl (see page 17)

•

1. Combine the carrots, onions, garlic, spices and sauces in a frying pan or wok with the ½ pint (300 ml) stock. Bring to the boil, then cover, reduce the heat, and simmer for 10–15 minutes. Uncover and simmer, stirring occasionally, for 5 minutes, until the vegetables are tender and glazed.

2. Meanwhile, combine the lentils with the unsalted stock or water in a large saucepan. Bring to the boil, then reduce the heat and leave to simmer, occasionally skimming foam from the surface.

3. Put the carrot and onion mixture in a blender with the red peppers, and blend until smooth. Stir into the lentils, and continue simmering until the lentils are tender. (They will need about 25 minutes' total cooking time.) Season with salt and pepper, a little vegetable bouillon powder, if you have used water, and more Tabasco and Worcestershire sauces as needed.

4. Purée (in small batches) in the blender until velvety smooth. Return to the pan, and reheat. Stir in the coriander.

5. Top each serving with a dab of Peach Salsa or hot mango chutney surrounded by Beetroot Swirl.

Pantry Chilli Bean Soup

MAKES 3¼ PINTS (1.8 litres)

NO SUBTLETY here. Open some cans, throw them together, cook for a few minutes, then purée half for an interesting texture. I think of this as chuck-wagon cooking: imagine cowboys sitting around their campfire, spooning this soup out of their tin bowls. And afterwards? Consult Mel Brooks for the answer.

■

1 large onion, chopped

3–4 dry-pack sundried tomatoes, chopped (use scissors)

4 black olives in brine, drained and slivered off their stones

2 garlic cloves, crushed

1–1½ teaspoons ground coriander (to taste)

1–1½ teaspoons ground cumin (to taste)

pinch or two of crushed dried chillies

1¼ pints (750 ml) stock

¼ pint (150 ml) red wine

two 15 oz (425 g) cans borlotti beans, drained and rinsed

15 oz (425 g) jar or can red peppers, drained and chopped

two 14 oz (400 g) cans chopped tomatoes

1 tablespoon tomato purée

salt and freshly ground pepper, to taste

4 tablespoons freshly grated Parmesan cheese (optional)

Tomato Salsa (see pages 18–19), to serve

■

1. Combine the onion, sundried tomatoes, olives, garlic, spices and chillies in a heavy-bottomed saucepan. Stir in ¼ pint (150 ml) stock and the wine. Cover and simmer briskly for 5–7 minutes. Uncover and simmer briskly for a further 3–5 minutes, until the onion is tender and the liquid has almost gone.

2. Stir in the beans, peppers, remaining stock, canned tomatoes, tomato purée and salt and pepper to taste. Simmer, partially covered, for 10–15 minutes. Cool slightly.

3. Purée half the soup in small batches in a blender. Combine the puréed and unpuréed portions, and stir in the grated cheese, if using. Bring to a simmer. Taste and adjust the seasoning.

4. Serve the soup, each bowlful topped with a generous tablespoon of salsa.

Cream of Cauliflower and Broccoli Soup

MAKES 3 PINTS (1.7 litres)

THAWED frozen cauliflower and broccoli are flabby, but because, in this recipe, they are cooked to tenderness, then puréed, it doesn't matter a jot. The taste isn't affected at all, in fact it's marvellous. Don't thaw the vegetables first, just throw them into the pan with the stock and seasonings.

2¼ lb (1 kg) pack frozen mixed cauliflower and broccoli florets
2¾ pints (1.6 litres) vegetable stock
salt and freshly ground pepper, to taste
Tabasco sauce, to taste
4 garlic cloves, crushed
1 red onion, chopped
1½ teaspoons dried tarragon

1½ teaspoons ground hot paprika
4–5 oz (125 g) tub Boursin Léger

To serve
Fresh Tomato Salsa (see page 18)
Chilli, Beetroot or White Bean Swirl (see pages 15–17)

---

1. Combine the vegetables and 2½ pints (1.4 litres) of the stock in a saucepan, season with salt and pepper and Tabasco, and simmer for 5–7 minutes, until thawed and tender.

2. Meanwhile, combine the garlic, onion, tarragon, paprika and remaining stock in a small frying pan, and simmer for approximately 10 minutes, until the onions are tender, and the liquid has about gone. Add to the vegetables.

3. Put some of the mixture in a blender with the Boursin Léger, and blend until very smooth. Pour into a clean saucepan.

4. Blend the remaining vegetables and stock in batches, and add to the first batch in the saucepan. Stir, season to taste with additional salt and pepper and Tabasco, and reheat.

5. Serve the soup in bowls, adding a dollop of salsa in the centre of each, surrounded by a spiral of Chilli, Beetroot or White Bean Swirl.

Curried Pea Soup

MAKES 2½ PINTS (1.4 litres)

PEAS freeze brilliantly; they don't lose colour and texture, and the taste really is (oh, dreaded cliché) 'garden fresh'. There is no need to thaw them first, but cook them quickly, so that they retain their colour and vibrant freshness.

12 spring onions, trimmed and sliced
½ inch (1 cm) piece fresh root ginger,
  peeled and crushed
2 tablespoons mild korma curry powder
1½ pints (900 ml) stock

¼ pint (150 ml) medium dry sherry
1¼ lb (550 g) frozen petits pois
salt and freshly ground pepper, to taste
hot mango chutney and White Bean
  Swirl (see page 16), to serve

1. Combine the onions, ginger, curry powder, ½ pint (300 ml) of the stock, and the sherry in a saucepan and simmer, uncovered, for approximately 10 minutes, until the onions are tender and the liquid greatly reduced.

2. Stir in the peas and remaining stock, and season with salt and pepper. Simmer for 3–4 minutes, until the peas are just cooked but remain bright green and fresh tasting.

3. Purée the soup in batches, in a blender, until smooth and velvety. Taste, and adjust the seasonings and temperature, if necessary.

4. Serve with a dollop of chutney in the centre of each bowlful, surrounded by the White Bean Swirl.

Aubergine–Cauliflower–Mushroom Soup

MAKES 3 PINTS (1.7 litres)

AUBERGINE is magical in soup. It provides a mysterious richness that teases the palate, but is very hard to identify. Along with the aubergine, a satisfying array of vegetables add their own character to this soup: mushrooms, peppers, cauliflower, red onion . . . The colour and the velvety smoothness of the final purée make it a soup to savour on the tongue, rather than to gulp down. Season it well; blandness would ruin it.

———— ∎ ————

8 oz (225 g) aubergine, trimmed, peeled and roughly chopped

1 large red onion, chopped

8 oz (225 g) mushrooms, thickly sliced

4 garlic cloves, crushed

4 black olives in brine, drained and slivered off their stones

3 dry-pack sundried tomatoes, chopped (use scissors)

pinch or two of crushed dried chillies (to taste)

salt and freshly ground pepper, to taste

4 fl oz (100 ml) dry red wine

2–3 dashes teriyaki sauce

2½ pints (1.4 litres) stock

1 cauliflower, trimmed and separated into florets

14 oz (400 g) can chopped tomatoes

15 oz (425 g) jar or can peppers, drained and chopped, or 4 char-grilled peppers (see page 9), peeled and chopped

Roasted Tomato Swirl (see page 17) and shredded fresh basil leaves, to garnish

———— ∎ ————

1. Combine the aubergine, onion, mushrooms, garlic, olives, sundried tomatoes, chillies, salt and pepper, wine, teriyaki and ½ pint (300 ml) of the stock in a non-stick wok or saucepan. Simmer, uncovered, for about 10 minutes, until the vegetables are tender and the liquid almost gone, stirring occasionally.

2. Add the cauliflower and cook, stirring for 2–3 minutes. Stir in the canned tomatoes, peppers and remaining stock, and simmer, uncovered, for approximately 15 minutes, until the cauliflower is tender. Taste and adjust the seasonings, if necessary. Cool slightly.

3. Purée the soup in batches in a blender until velvety smooth. Return to the pan and reheat briefly.

4. Top each serving with a spoonful of Roasted Tomato Swirl and a scattering of basil.

Tomato Ragout

MAKES 3½–4 PINTS (2–2.3 litres)

WHAT would we do without canned tomato products? This is an instant soup/ragout, conjured up out of the pantry, that I like to make early in the week and then dip into for quick meals and pick-me-ups. It's one of those store-cupboard recipes that delivers maximum comfort for minimum effort. Sometimes I add drained canned broad beans and/or drained, quartered canned artichoke hearts in step three. When I'm trying to lose weight I live on this ragout, raw vegetables, and matzo crackers spread with quark, a dab of *sambal oelek*, and a topping of sliced ripe vine tomatoes. It's a feast, not a punishment!

— ∎ —

four 14 oz (400 g) cans whole Italian
  tomatoes
pinch or two of crushed dried chillies
  (optional)
15 oz (425 g) jar or can red peppers in
  brine (optional)
a few dry-pack sundried tomatoes,
  coarsely chopped

2–3 black olives in brine, drained and
  slivered off their stones
freshly ground pepper, to taste
2–3 tablespoons tomato purée
handful of fresh parsley, chopped
a few fresh basil leaves, shredded (if you
  have them)

— ∎ —

1. Tip the tomatoes, juice and all, into a non-reactive saucepan, and roughly crush them with a potato masher. Sprinkle in the chillies.

2. Drain the liquid from the pepper can or jar, if using. With a pair of kitchen scissors, roughly chop the peppers while they are still in the jar or can. Tip them in with the tomatoes. Add the sundried tomatoes and olives, and bring to the boil.

3. Reduce the heat and simmer for about 10 minutes. Season with pepper and simmer for 10 minutes more. Stir in the tomato purée and simmer for 5–10 minutes more, until thick. Stir in the chopped parsley and shredded basil, if available.

Spinach Soup

MAKES 1½ PINTS (900 ml)

A S WITH frozen peas, it is important to cook frozen spinach quickly, so that it remains bright green. Overcooked spinach turns a horribly bilious drab olive, and is most unappetising.

---

1 large all-purpose potato (approximately 12 oz/350 g), peeled and cut into chunks
1 pint (600 ml) stock
salt and freshly ground pepper, to taste

1 lb (450 g) frozen chopped spinach (unthawed)
¼–½ teaspoon freshly grated nutmeg
4–5 oz (125 g) tub Boursin Léger

---

1. Combine the potato and stock in a saucepan, season with salt and pepper, and simmer for 5–7 minutes, until half cooked.

2. Stir in the frozen spinach and continue simmering for another 5–7 minutes, until both the potato and spinach are cooked. The spinach should remain bright green. Cool slightly, and season with grated nutmeg and more salt and pepper, if necessary.

3. Purée in batches in a blender with the Boursin Léger. Reheat and serve.

Hot and Sour Soup

MAKES 2 PINTS (1.1 litres)

N OW THAT all kinds of Oriental ingredients are available in virtually every supermarket, this – one of the most delicious of Chinese soups – can become a speciality of your own kitchen. The problem with Hot and Sour Soup from many restaurants and take-aways is that it never seems to be either hot enough or sour enough, and it often resembles a liquid repository for a lot of rather tired ingredients. This one is vibrant, fresh and as hot and sour as you want it to be. Use the left-over bamboo shoots in a mixed salad. Cube the left-over tofu and use it in place of prawns in Prawn Noodle Soup (see page 40) or chicken in Chicken Soup with Lime, Coriander and Tortilla Strips (see page 41) – perfect for vegetarians if you also omit the Thai fish sauce from the former.

2 oz (50 g) shredded very lean pork
1 teaspoon medium dry sherry
1 teaspoon cornflour
1½ pints (900 ml) chicken stock
1 tablespoon tomato purée
4 shiitake mushrooms, trimmed of their
  stems and sliced
6 button mushrooms (approximately
  2 oz/50 g), sliced
2 oz (50 g) canned bamboo shoots,
  drained and cut into thin strips
2 oz (50 g) tofu, drained, blotted dry and
  shredded

3 tablespoons cider vinegar
1 tablespoon soy sauce
¾ teaspoon ground white pepper (or
  more, to taste)
½ teaspoon Thai fish sauce
2 egg whites
3 tablespoons cornflour, dissolved in
  4 fl oz (100 ml) water
salt (if needed)

To serve
2–3 spring onions, trimmed and chopped
sesame oil–water spray (see page 8)

1. Put the pork strips, sherry and 1 teaspoon cornflour in a small bowl, stir together, and set aside.

2. Combine the stock and tomato purée in a wok or saucepan and bring to the boil.

3. Put both kinds of mushrooms and the bamboo shoots into a small bowl.

4. In yet another bowl, combine the tofu, vinegar, soy sauce, pepper and fish sauce.

5. Finally, put the egg whites in a bowl and beat lightly (do *not* beat until foamy).

6. Now you are ready to cook the soup! Stir the pork strips and their juices into the boiling stock. Cook, stirring, for 30 seconds. Add the mushrooms and bamboo shoots, and cook, stirring, for 1 minute.

7. Stir in the tofu mixture and bring back to the boil. Stir in the cornflour and water mixture and stir until the soup thickens (less than 1 minute). Slowly pour the egg whites into the boiling soup, stirring all the time, to form 'egg flowers' (essentially, scrambled egg whites). Taste and add salt if necessary, along with a little more pepper and/or vinegar to achieve the hot and sour taste that pleases you.

8. Ladle the soup into bowls and top each serving with a spoonful of spring onion pieces and a good spritz of the sesame oil–water spray.

Prawn Noodle Soup

MAKES 2½ PINTS (1.4 litres)

ANOTHER Oriental soup – Thai this time – that takes advantage of the rich Oriental pickings in our supermarkets. For a change, substitute sliced Roasted Pork Tenderloin (see page 96) for the prawns. Slice it, and perch a few slices on top of each bowlful of soup.

———— ■ ————

12 spring onions, trimmed
handful of fresh coriander
1–2 chillies, deseeded and finely chopped
3 garlic cloves, crushed
½ inch (1 cm) piece fresh root ginger,
  peeled and crushed
juice and grated rind of 1 lime

3 pints (1.7 litres) stock
½ teaspoon Thai fish sauce
several dashes of teriyaki sauce
8 oz (225 g) vermicelli or angel hair pasta
  (very fine spaghetti)
1 stalk lemon grass
8 oz (225 g) tiny cooked, peeled prawns

———— ■ ————

1. Slice the white bulbs of the spring onions. Slice the green parts and set aside for later. Separate the coriander leaves from the stems, and chop the stems. Chop the leaves and set aside.

2. Combine the white spring onion slices with the chillies, garlic, ginger, *half* the lime juice and grated rind, the chopped *stems* of the coriander, ½ pint (300 ml) of the stock, and the fish and teriyaki sauces in a heavy-bottomed saucepan. Cover, bring to the boil, and boil for 7–10 minutes. Uncover and simmer briskly for approximately 5 minutes, until the garlic and onions are gently 'frying' in the syrupy juices.

3. When the onion is tender, stir in the pasta, lemon grass, remaining stock, and remaining lime juice and rind. Simmer, uncovered, for 5 minutes until the pasta is tender, stirring occasionally.

4. Remove the pan from the heat. Take out and discard the lemon grass stalk, and stir in the prawns, chopped coriander leaves and sliced spring onion greens. Return to the heat, and stir for a moment or two to heat through, then serve.

Chicken Soup with Lime, Coriander and Tortilla Strips

MAKES 3½ PINTS (2.1 litres)

A MEXICAN fiesta in a bowl, this colourful main-course soup is filled with pizzazz. Don't make it ahead of time; if left to sit, it loses its signature freshness, and the chicken loses its creamy texture and becomes stringy.

■

4 black olives in brine, drained and slivered off their stones

1 red onion, chopped

2 garlic cloves, crushed

3 dry-pack sundried tomatoes, chopped (use scissors)

1 chilli, deseeded and chopped

½ tablespoon ground cumin

½ tablespoon ground coriander

2 pints (1.1 litres) chicken or vegetable stock

2 chicken breast fillets, skinned and cut into 1 inch (2.5 cm) pieces

ground paprika, to taste

salt and freshly ground pepper, to taste

12 oz (350 g) can extra-sweet corn kernels, drained

4 'flavour' tomatoes, peeled, deseeded and diced

4 tablespoons chopped fresh coriander

juice of 2 limes (approximately 2 fl oz/ 50 ml)

2–3 corn tortillas, cut into strips (see Note below)

■

1. Combine the olives, onion, garlic, sundried tomatoes, chilli, spices and 4 fl oz (100 ml) of the stock in a non-stick wok or saucepan. Cover, bring to the boil, and boil for 5 minutes. Uncover, reduce the heat, and simmer for 3–5 minutes, until the onions are tender and the onions and spices are gently 'frying' in their own juices.

2. Toss the chicken with paprika and salt and pepper.

3. Add the chicken to the onion and garlic mixture, stir, and cook for 2 minutes. Stir in the remaining stock, the corn and tomatoes, and season with salt and pepper. Bring to the boil, then reduce the heat and simmer for 3–4 minutes, until the chicken is just done. Stir in the coriander, lime juice and tortilla strips, and serve at once.

Note

To prepare the tortilla strips, heat a heavy-bottomed frying pan or ridged 'grill' pan until very hot. Dry-fry the tortillas (one or two at a time, depending on the pan) for 30–40 seconds on each side, until pliable. Cut into ½ inch (1 cm) wide strips with scissors.

· CHAPTER 3 ·

Take a Packet of . . .

THE problem with ready-to-eat packet meals lies in dreadful boredom. Slamming a ready-made meal into the microwave or the cooker involves no personal input whatsoever. It always tastes the same, someone else (an anonymous, corporate someone) decided on the colour, texture and seasonings, and the portion size is usually ludicrous (too small!). It's just like that old joke: 'The food was awful – and the portions were *so small!*'

So forget packet *meals*, and downsize to much more basic packets. Here is where the store-cupboard comes into its own. All those comforting packets of carbohydrate, waiting to be boiled, soaked or steeped, combined with a quick sauce or some interesting vegetables, and feasted upon – what luxury! Take a packet of pasta, gnocchi, bulghur, couscous, polenta or even instant potato, and create yourself a satisfying, intensely personal meal in minutes.

PASTA AND NOODLES

Pasta is true convenience food. While the water boils, and then while the pasta cooks, the timing is just right to whip together an elegant little sauce (or even a larger vulgar one). Low-fat sauces are easy: the stock sauté flavour infusion, low-fat dairy products, canned tomatoes – all of these make low-fat sauces simple to prepare and a pleasure to eat.

Alfredo Sauce for Pasta

MAKES 22 fl oz (650 ml); ENOUGH FOR UP TO 1 lb (450 g) PASTA
(uncooked weight)

SOMEONE once called genuine Pasta Alfredo 'a heart attack on a plate'. Needless to say, my version isn't. To make the real thing, you would need large quantities of butter, double cream and cheese. My combination of quark and fromage frais, along with the intense cheese taste of Parmesan, enfolds the pasta in gloriously creamy melted cheesy richness, *without* the fat. This version (compared to the scary original) saves you approximately 400 Calories and 25 grams of fat *per serving*! In addition to saucing pasta, it makes a very special sandwich spread or dip, or try it on hot toast.

———— ∎ ————

7 oz (200 g) carton quark
11 fl oz (325 ml) very low fat fromage
   frais

2–3 oz (50–75 g) Parmesan cheese,
   grated
salt and freshly ground pepper, to taste

———— ∎ ————

Combine the ricotta, fromage frais and Parmesan in a food processor, or blender, and process until very well mixed. Season with salt (if it needs it) and plenty of freshly ground pepper. Fold into freshly cooked pasta.

Variations

- Process in as much pan-braised garlic (see page 10) as you like, and some chopped fresh herbs, in step 1.
- Fold in strips of smoked salmon.
- Dollop some tomato sauce (see page 28) on top of each serving of creamy pasta, and strew on some fresh herbs.

Aubergine and Ham Sauce for Pasta

MAKES 2 PINTS (1.1 litres); ENOUGH FOR UP TO 18 OZ (500 g) PASTA
(uncooked weight)

ONLY a small amount of smoked ham is used in this recipe, but, if it is of top quality, it will be enough to imbue the aubergine with its smokiness. The aubergine and onion become so tender that they almost melt.

———— ∎ ————

1 large red onion, roughly chopped
12 oz (350 g) aubergine, trimmed,
   peeled and cut into ½ inch (1 cm)
   cubes
2 garlic cloves, crushed
3 dry-pack sundried tomatoes, chopped
   (use scissors)
4 black olives in brine, drained and slivered off their stones
4 fl oz (100 ml) dry red wine

½ pint (300 ml) stock
14 oz (400 g) can chopped tomatoes
15 oz (425 g) jar or can red peppers,
   drained and chopped, or 4 char-grilled
   peppers (see page 9), peeled and
   chopped
4 fl oz (100 ml) passata
3 oz (75 g) smoked ham, slivered or diced
salt and freshly ground pepper, to taste
2–3 tablespoons shredded basil leaves

———— ∎ ————

1. Combine the onion, aubergine, garlic, sundried tomatoes, olives, wine and stock in a heavy-bottomed frying pan. Cover and simmer briskly for 7–10 minutes. Uncover and simmer for a further 5–10 minutes, until the onion and aubergine are meltingly tender.

2. Stir in the tomatoes, peppers, passata and ham. Season as needed with salt and pepper (the amount of salt needed will depend on the saltiness of the ham). Simmer, uncovered, for 7–10 minutes, until thick and savoury. Stir in the basil and serve with freshly cooked pasta.

New Potato and Mint Sauce for Pasta

MAKES 1 PINT (600 ml); ENOUGH FOR UP TO 12 OZ (350 g) PASTA
(uncooked weight)

I TASTED several different pasta sauces containing potatoes and fresh herbs in Italy, and I thought the high-carbohydrate combination of pasta and potato was brilliant.

— • —

4 black olives in brine, drained and
  slivered off their stones
4–5 dry-pack sundried tomatoes, coarsely
  chopped (use scissors)
3 garlic cloves, crushed
1 onion, roughly chopped
pinch or two of crushed dried chillies
10 tiny new potatoes, halved

½ pint (300 ml) stock
14 oz (400 g) can chopped tomatoes,
  whirled in the blender until smooth
salt and freshly ground pepper, to taste
1 tablespoon tomato purée
2 tablespoons chopped fresh parsley
2 tablespoons shredded fresh mint

— • —

1. Combine the olives, sundried tomatoes, garlic, onion, chilli, potatoes and stock in a heavy-bottomed non-reactive frying pan. Cover and boil for 7–10 minutes. Uncover and simmer briskly, stirring occasionally, for a further 5 minutes, until the onion and potatoes are 'frying' in their own juices, and the onion is tender.

2. Pour in the tomatoes and season to taste with salt and freshly ground pepper. Simmer for approximately 10 minutes. Stir in the tomato purée and simmer for 5 minutes more. Stir in the herbs. Serve tossed into freshly cooked and drained pasta.

Tomato–Chilli–Garlic Sauce

MAKES 2 PINTS (1.1 litres); ENOUGH FOR UP TO 18 OZ
(500 g) PASTA (uncooked weight)

THE GARLIC in this lively tomato sauce variation takes on a mellow taste and melting texture. Serve with pasta or other grains. Alternatively, serve it with grilled lean beef (fillet or skirt), or use it on a polenta pizza (see page 56).

■

10 garlic cloves, halved lengthwise
1 chilli, deseeded and finely chopped
3–4 black olives in brine, drained and slivered off their stones
4–5 dry-pack sundried tomatoes, diced (use scissors)
4 fl oz (100 ml) stock
2–3 fl oz (50–75 ml) dry red wine

two 14 oz (400 g) cans chopped tomatoes
4–5 large fresh ripe tomatoes, peeled, cored, deseeded and roughly chopped
salt and freshly ground pepper, to taste
1–2 tablespoons tomato purée
4–5 fresh basil leaves, shredded

■

1. Combine the garlic, chilli, olives, sundried tomatoes, stock and wine in a heavy-bottomed non-reactive frying pan. Simmer, uncovered, for 7–10 minutes, until the garlic is very tender and the liquid almost gone. Don't let it burn – add more stock during the cooking, if necessary.

2. Stir in the canned tomatoes, and simmer for 5–7 minutes. Add the fresh tomatoes and season with salt and pepper. Simmer for 5–7 minutes more, then stir in the tomato purée and basil. Let simmer for another 5 minutes, then serve with freshly cooked pasta or other grains.

Spring Onion and Pea Sauce for Pasta

MAKES 1½ PINTS (900 ml); ENOUGH FOR UP TO 12 OZ (350 g) PASTA
(uncooked weight)

EXQUISITELY fresh-tasting (blessed frozen peas), this sauce is best tossed, freshly made, into just-cooked pasta shapes. Unlike the previous tomato-based sauces, this one has no tomatoes, won't be as good on the second day as it is freshly made, and does not freeze. Shells are the pasta shapes of choice here, so that some of the peas and other bits get trapped in the crevices. When you sauce the pasta, add a few spoonfuls of the pasta cooking water.

———— • ————

25 spring onions, trimmed and thinly sliced
2–3 garlic cloves, crushed
4–5 black olives in brine, drained and slivered off their stones
1 teaspoon brine from olive jar

juice of 1 lemon
1 pint (600 ml) stock
1 lb (450 g) very fresh peas, or 12 oz (350 g) frozen peas, thawed
3 tablespoons shredded fresh mint leaves
freshly ground pepper, to taste

———— • ————

1. Combine the onions, garlic, olives, olive brine, half the lemon juice and half the stock in a heavy-bottomed frying pan. Cover and boil for 5–7 minutes. Uncover and simmer for a further 7–10 minutes, until the onions and garlic are tender and the liquid is almost gone.

2. Add the peas and the remaining lemon juice and stock. Simmer for 3–4 minutes, until the peas are just tender. Stir in the mint and season with pepper. Serve with freshly cooked pasta shells.

Chinese Prawns and Mushrooms with Noodles

SERVES 4

A S WITH all Chinese cookery, the secret is to have the ingredients prepared and efficiently set out on your work surface next to the cooker. Once everything is chopped and ready, the actual cooking takes no time at all.

■

Prawns
1 lb (450 g) tiger prawns, peeled and
  deveined (see Note, below)
4 fl oz (100 ml) fish stock
2 tablespoons medium dry sherry
1 teaspoon teriyaki sauce
½ red chilli, deseeded and chopped
½ green chilli, deseeded and chopped
2 garlic cloves, crushed
1 inch (2.5 cm) piece fresh root ginger,
  peeled and crushed
6 spring onions, trimmed and sliced (the
  white, and a few inches of the green)

Mushrooms
5 oz (135 g) shiitake mushrooms,
  trimmed of their stems and quartered

5 oz (135 g) brown-cap mushrooms,
  quartered
4 fl oz (100 ml) vegetable stock
2 fl oz (50 ml) medium dry sherry
2 teaspoons teriyaki sauce
salt and freshly ground pepper, to taste
1 tablespoon cornflour, whisked into 3
  tablespoons cold water

To Serve
⅔ package (approximately 4 oz/110 g)
  Chinese thread egg noodles
chopped fresh coriander

■

1. Put a large pan of salted water on to boil (or boil in a kettle first to save time). Combine the prawn ingredients in a bowl, and set aside.

2. Combine all the mushroom ingredients, *except* the cornflour and water, in a wok. Stir-fry over high heat for 4–6 minutes, until the mushrooms are tender and have exuded quite a bit of liquid.

3. Stir in the cornflour liquid, and cook, stirring, for a minute or so, until thickened. Scrape into a bowl, and rinse out the wok.

4. Put the noodles into the boiling water, turn off the heat, cover and leave for 3 minutes, stirring occasionally.

5. Meanwhile, tip the prawns and their marinade into the wok. Stir and cook over the highest heat for about 3 minutes, until the prawns are pink, curled and *just* done. Tip in the mushroom mixture and stir to combine and heat through.

6. Drain the noodles and tip into a warm bowl. Toss in the prawn and mushroom mixture and sprinkle with coriander.

Note

To devein a prawn, peel it, then cut a slit along its back with a small, sharp knife. Rinse under cold water and remove the unsightly black vein.

Gnocchi

Gnocchi are tender potato and wheat flour dumplings; the most delicious little fat-free morsels you can imagine. Packet gnocchi (look in the pasta section of your supermarket) are superb and *very* quick to prepare; simply boil up a panful of lightly salted water, drop in the gnocchi (be careful of hot splashes), and boil until they rise to the surface. Skim them out, and mix with tomato sauce (see page 28) or any of the pasta sauces on pages 43–47. Sprinkle with fresh herbs and serve. It is one of the most comforting fast meals possible. For a change, sprinkle some grated Parmesan or shredded half-fat mozzarella on top, flash under the grill to melt, and serve.

Pasta with Prawns and Rocket

SERVES 3–4

THIS sauce is extremely fast and extremely fresh. Prawns cook in the blink of an eye (if they overcook they turn mealy), and the tomatoes and rocket are almost not cooked at all. The hot pasta with the barely cooked peppery rocket, the intensely flavoured tomatoes, and the just-cooked prawns make a perfect summer meal.

•

12 oz (350 g) dried penne
¾ pint (450 ml) stock
3 fl oz (75 ml) dry white wine
4 garlic cloves, crushed
generous pinch of crushed dried chillies
4 dry-pack sundried tomatoes, chopped (use scissors)
4 black olives in brine, drained and slivered off their stones
several dashes of Tabasco sauce

several dashes of Worcestershire sauce
8 oz (225 g) tiger prawns, peeled and deveined (see Note, page 49)
4 tablespoons fresh basil strips
1 tablespoon fresh mint strips
1 lb (450 g) firm but ripe vine tomatoes, cut into quarters and deseeded
1½ oz (40 g) pack of rocket
salt and freshly ground pepper
chopped fresh parsley, to garnish

•

1. Cook the pasta in plenty of salted, boiling water for 8–10 minutes, until *al dente* (just tender, not mushy).

2. While it cooks, prepare the sauce. Combine ½ pint (300 ml) of the stock with the wine, garlic, chilli, sundried tomatoes, olives and sauces in a frying pan, and boil for 7–10 minutes, until the liquid is almost gone. Add the remaining stock and the prawns, stir, and cook for 2–4 minutes, until the prawns are just cooked (pink and beginning to curl). Stir in the basil, mint, fresh tomatoes and rocket, and cook for a few seconds. Season with salt and pepper.

3. Drain the pasta, put it into a warm bowl, and toss with the prawn and tomato mixture. Sprinkle with parsley and serve at once.

Open Ravioli with Mushrooms and Goat's Cheese–Tomato Sauce

MAKES 2

FOR OPEN ravioli you will need fresh lasagne sheets, available in many supermarkets. This recipe serves two, but you can multiply the quantities to feed as many as you wish, although you will not need to double the mushrooms; each ravioli does not need to be filled quite so lavishly. I love this lazy person's version of ravioli (rather like free-form lasagne). It's ridiculously simple, yet it makes a dramatic presentation. If you have no tomato sauce on hand, use Sugocasa (bottled, seasoned chopped tomatoes) or passata, along with the goat's cheese, Tabasco sauce and olives in step 1.

▪

4 fl oz (100 ml) Ten-Minute Tomato Sauce (see page 28)
2½ oz (65 g) medium-fat goat's cheese
a dash or two of Tabasco sauce
2 black olives in brine, drained and slivered off their stones (optional)

2 sheets of fresh lasagne
½ quantity Creamy Mushroom Ragout (see page 112), warmed
chopped fresh parsley and torn fresh basil leaves, to serve

▪

1. Combine the tomato sauce and goat's cheese with the Tabasco and olives, if using, in a blender, and purée until smooth. Put into a saucepan and heat gently.

2. Meanwhile, cook the lasagne sheets according to the package directions (it should take about 3 minutes). Cut each in half to make four squares or rectangles.

3. Quickly put a lasagne piece on each of two warm plates. Spoon half the mushrooms over each, so that they lavishly overflow the pasta. Top each with a second sheet, turning it slightly so that it is at a different angle. Pour half the sauce over each one, so that it covers part of the top and overflows and encircles the ravioli. Quickly sprinkle with parsley and torn basil and serve at once.

Other Suggestions for Open Ravioli Fillings

Spicy Ratatouille (see page 109); Aubergine and Ham Sauce (see page 44); Rosemary Prawns (see page 71)

BULGHUR

Bulghur is pre-cooked cracked wheat. To prepare, simply cover with boiling water and let stand for 30 minutes. The classic bulghur dish is tabbouleh, for which the soaked bulghur is combined with lots of fresh mint, parsley, lemon juice and tomato. Here, tabbouleh is given a good dose of turn-of-the-twentieth century multi-ethnicity.

Tabbouleh with Attitude

MAKES 2½ PINTS (1.4 litres)

8 fl oz (225 ml) stock
4 fl oz (100 ml) passata
1 teaspoon ground coriander
1 teaspoon ground cumin
several dashes of Tabasco sauce
several dashes of Worcestershire sauce
salt and freshly ground pepper, to taste
5½ oz (160 g) bulghur
1 small red onion, chopped
2 garlic cloves, crushed
½ large cucumber, peeled, halved lengthwise, deseeded and chopped
juice of 1 orange, 1 lime and ½ lemon

1 tablespoon balsamic vinegar
12 oz (350 g) can extra-sweet sweetcorn kernels, drained
6 vine tomatoes, halved, deseeded and coarsely chopped
1 red or yellow pepper, cored, deseeded, peeled (see page 9) and chopped, or 1 char-grilled pepper (see page 9), peeled and chopped, or 1 canned pepper, chopped
4 tablespoons chopped fresh parsley
2 tablespoons chopped fresh coriander
2 tablespoons shredded fresh mint

1. Combine the stock, passata, ground spices, Tabasco and Worcestershire sauces, salt and pepper in a saucepan and bring to the boil. Remove from the heat, stir into the bulghur in a large bowl, and let stand for about 30 minutes until tender.

2. Meanwhile, in a non-reactive bowl, combine the onion, garlic, cucumber, citrus juices and vinegar.

3. When the bulghur is tender, fold in the vegetables and the onion–garlic mixture. Combine well with two spoons, and mix in the herbs. Taste and adjust the seasonings, adding salt, pepper and Tabasco as needed.

COUSCOUS

Couscous is made up of tiny grain-like bits of semolina wheat. When cooked, it forms a comforting, tender, wheaty mound, resembling a cross between rice and very small pasta.

Basic Couscous

MAKES 1 PINT (600 ml)

PRE-COOKED couscous takes ten minutes to prepare. All you need to do is pour on boiling liquid (stock, for flavour) and leave it alone. A mound of couscous nestles nicely next to the tomato-based sauces in the pasta section, particularly the Aubergine and Ham Sauce (see page 44) or the Tomato–Chilli–Garlic Sauce (see page 46). Couscous is also the perfect companion to any of the vegetable or bean stews (see pages 106–109).

————— ▪ —————

5 oz (135 g) pre-cooked couscous
8 fl oz (225 ml) very well seasoned
boiling stock

————— ▪ —————

Put the couscous in a bowl and stir in the boiling stock. Cover and let stand for 10 minutes, until the couscous is tender and the liquid is absorbed. Fluff with a fork.

Fish Couscous

MAKES 1½ PINTS (900 ml)

FISH and couscous are exceedingly good partners, especially when highly seasoned. This particular combo resonates with chilli, garlic and citrus. With a drizzle of dark dressing zigzagging over the pale, herb-flecked couscous, it looks amazing.

———— • ————

4 oz (110 g) cod fillet, oven-poached (see page 67)

1 pint (600 ml) Basic Couscous (see page 53)

Spicy Thai Dressing (see page 76)

chopped fresh coriander and parsley, and lemon and lime wedges, to serve

———— • ————

1. Flake the fish and mix gently into the couscous with all the fish cooking juices. Spread on a platter.

2. Drizzle with the dressing, strew on the herbs, and surround with lemon and lime wedges.

POLENTA

Polenta, a sort of savoury porridge of yellow maize meal, is one of the most comforting foods in the world. It is a staple of northern Italy and the Swiss Ticino (and eaten in many other parts of the world under different names). To cook polenta, maize meal is stirred into boiling liquid until it is softly set and the mixture pulls away from the sides of the pan (the texture is not unlike that of mashed potatoes). Traditionally, polenta is slo-o-ow food – 40 minutes of arduous, elbow-breaking stirring – but quick-cooking polenta (look for it in large supermarkets and speciality delis) is readily available. It cooks in less than ten minutes and, although purists insist that it is not *de rigueur*, is supremely comforting, and exceedingly (if seasoned well) delicious.

The secret of good polenta cookery is to avoid blandness. Cook in a well-seasoned stock, rather than water, and add plenty of flavour ingredients.

Polenta

FILLS FOUR 14 oz (400 g) CANS (see Notes, page 56)

WITH polenta, seasoning is all. Stir the polenta in stock that has been seasoned with the olive–sundried tomato infusion used in this recipe, and the dish will be saturated with flavour. Left-over polenta is pure treasure (see the suggestions overleaf), but, if you wish, the recipe can be halved or even quartered: reduce the amount of polenta and stock, but leave the infusion as it is. Serve with any of the tomato-based sauces (see Chapter 1 and pages 44–46 in this chapter), or see the suggestions overleaf.

·

Infusion
1 red onion, diced
4 dry-pack sundried tomatoes, chopped (use scissors)
4 black olives in brine, drained and slivered off their stones
1 chilli, deseeded and chopped
pinch of crushed dried chillies
2 garlic cloves, crushed
4 fl oz (100 ml) red wine

½ pint (300 ml) stock

Polenta
2½ pints (1.4 litres) stock
salt and freshly ground pepper, to taste
13 oz (375 g) box quick-cooking polenta
2 tablespoons chopped fresh parsley
2 tablespoons chopped fresh basil
2–3 tablespoons freshly grated Parmesan cheese (optional)

·

1. For the infusion, combine the onion, sundried tomatoes, olives, fresh and dried chilli, garlic, wine and ½ pint (300 ml) stock in a large saucepan. Simmer briskly for 7–10 minutes, until the onion is tender and the liquid about gone.

2. Add 2½ pints (1.4 litres) stock, and season with a generous amount of salt and pepper. Bring to just below the boil and gradually add the polenta in a slow, steady stream, stirring well with a whisk as you do so. (Wear an oven glove to protect your arm from searing splatters.) Cook, stirring, for 5–7 minutes, until smooth, switching to a wooden spoon as it thickens. The polenta will bubble volcanically, so be careful. Towards the end of cooking, stir in the herbs, the grated cheese, if using, and more salt and pepper if needed.

Variation

Broccoli Polenta
Cook some frozen broccoli and chop it. Add with the stock in step 2.

Notes

To Store Cooked Polenta

To store polenta for the next day, or later in the week, spread the freshly cooked polenta on to a baking sheet, spoon it into a loaf tin or baking dish, or spoon into empty, clean food cans (tomato cans, for instance). Cool, cover and refrigerate. When you are ready to use the polenta, it will unmould perfectly from its pan or can.

To Heat Cooked, Chilled Polenta

1. Cut the polenta into squares, or slice it into rounds if it is moulded in a tomato can. Put it in a small baking dish and cover with foil for the conventional oven, or microwave cling film for the microwave.

2. Heat in the conventional oven at 180°C, 350°F, Gas Mark 4 for approximately 30 minutes, or in the microwave on Full Power for 6 minutes. If you have used the microwave, pierce the cling film with a sharp knife to release the steam, then carefully uncover.

To Grill Cooked, Chilled Polenta

1. Preheat the grill to its highest setting. Cover the grill tray with foil, shiny side up. Cut squares or rounds of polenta and place on the tray. Spray with oil–water spray (see page 8).

2. Grill, close to the heat, for approximately 2 minutes, until speckled with brown. Turn (spray lightly) and grill for a minute or two on the second side.

Things to do with Polenta

1. Use it to make pizza. Spread half the quantity of freshly cooked polenta on a non-stick 15 × 10 inch (38 × 25 cm) baking sheet, smoothing the top and building up the sides. Spread with tomato sauce (see page 28), arrange strips of grilled pepper and aubergine on top, and sprinkle with shredded half-fat Italian-style mozzarella. Grill until the cheese melts.

2. Cover slices of polenta with one of the bean stews (see pages 103, 104 and 106), top with shredded half-fat mozzarella and grill.

3. Serve it smothered with Glazed Mushroom (see page 65).

4. Layer it with grilled aubergine, courgettes and peppers, top with grated Parmesan cheese and bake or grill.

MASHED POTATO FLAKES

Thousands of years ago, the Incas stored potatoes by freeze-drying them, so the notion of instant potatoes is not exactly a modern one. A packet of potato flakes lurking in the cupboard is a fast and comforting dish waiting to happen. Do be sure to buy the unseasoned flakes (e.g. Mr Mash or Waitrose own brand), not the little pellets, and not the brands that have seasonings (and fat!) already added. Reconstitute the flakes in stock, rather than water, and add seasoning to your taste. Use the flakes for Potato Cakes (below) or Smoky Fish Cakes (see page 72).

Potato Cakes

MAKES 8

CRUSTY and cheesy with a lovely fluffy interior, these homely potato cakes are spectacular as a main dish with a spicy tomato or chilli sauce and salad.

—— ∎ ——

18 fl oz (500 ml) well-seasoned stock
4½ oz (120 g) sachet instant potato flakes
2 tablespoons each of fromage frais,
  Boursin Léger and freshly grated
  Parmesan cheese

salt and freshly ground pepper, to taste
flour for coating
plain breadcrumbs, seasoned
2 egg whites, lightly beaten
oil–water spray (see page 8)

—— ∎ ——

1. Put the stock in a large saucepan and bring to the boil. Remove from the heat and stir in the potato flakes. Let stand for a moment, then stir well. Stir in the fromage frais, Boursin Léger and Parmesan cheese, then taste and season with salt and pepper if necessary. Spread the mixture on a plate and put it in the freezer for a few minutes to cool off.

2. Meanwhile, put some flour, breadcrumbs and the egg whites on three separate plates. Preheat the grill, and line the grill tray with foil, shiny side up. Lightly spray the foil with oil and water spray.

3. When the grill is hot, form the potato mixture into 8 round patties, and flatten. Dip each in flour, then egg, and finally breadcrumbs, coating well. Place on the grill tray and spray lightly with oil and water spray.

4. Grill, 5 inches (12.5 cm) from the heat, for 2–3 minutes per side. They will brown, puff up, and smell divine. Serve with Ten-Minute Tomato Sauce (see page 28) or Chilli Sauce (see page 15).

· CHAPTER 4 ·

Fish

Long cooking spoils fish – it turns tough, dry and fibrous. Fish should be cooked for 9–10 minutes (at a high heat) per inch (2.5 cm) of thickness. (Exact timing depends on the thickness of your pans, and the performance of your hob and oven.) This timing ensures that the fish is *just* cooked and at its moist, delicate, pearly, translucent best. Make sure that the fish you buy is fresh (or fresh frozen), in other words don't buy it if it smells 'fishy'.

Even fatty fish is relatively low in calories, and fish fat is believed to be particularly heart healthy. The main problem with fish and shellfish is availability – often the selection in supermarkets is rather limited. However with even basics like cod, salmon, haddock, sole etc, wonderful quick meals are possible.

OPPOSITE Goat's Cheese Salad with Golden Spice Pan-Roasted Potatoes (pages 117 and 118), served with Artichoke and Cranberry Relish (page 20)

Overleaf: Salmon Fillet with Spinach (page 59) served with Olive and Cherry Tomato Relish (page 21) and a baked potato topped with Mango and Pepper Mayo (page 27)

Salmon fillet with Spinach

SERVES 1

THE TEXTURE of fresh salmon, when it is *just* cooked and sweetly moist, is one of the greatest of gastronomic pleasures. The farmed salmon available now beautifully delivers this pleasure, but its taste, compared with wild salmon, tends towards blandness, therefore it pays to set the fish against some lively seasoning. Here, salmon fillets rest on a bed of quickly cooked spinach that has been flavoured with a garlic, sundried tomato and olive infusion. The salmon, in this recipe and the next, is quickly seared on both sides, then, after the spinach (or Chinese leaves in the following recipe) is done, the fish is finished off in the residual heat of the pan. This method guarantees exquisitely moist fish.

---

5 oz (150 g) salmon fillet, skinned
salt and freshly ground pepper, to taste
olive oil–water spray (see page 8)
½ red onion, chopped
3 dry-pack sundried tomatoes, chopped
* (use scissors)*
3 black olives in brine, drained and sliv-
* ered off their stones*

2 garlic cloves, crushed
6 fl oz (175 ml) stock
8 oz (225 g) spinach
1 scant tablespoon tomato purée
chopped fresh mint, to serve

---

1. Season the salmon fillet with salt and pepper. Spray a heavy-bottomed non-stick frying pan with olive oil–water spray and sear the fillet on both sides until browned, just 1½ minutes in all. Set aside on a plate.

2. In the same pan, combine the onion, sundried tomatoes, olives, garlic and 4 fl oz (100 ml) of the stock. Cook for 3–4 minutes, until the liquid is about gone and the onions and garlic are 'frying' in their own juices and have lost their rawness.

3. Cram the spinach into the pan with the remaining stock. Cover and cook for 3–4 minutes, until the leaves are limp and cooked, then season with salt and pepper and stir in the tomato purée. Return the salmon to the pan, clap on the lid, and remove the pan from the heat. Leave to stand for 4–5 minutes, until the salmon is *just* done. Serve sprinkled with chopped mint.

Teriyaki Salmon with Chinese Leaves

SERVES 1

GIVE salmon an Oriental character with teriyaki, sherry, ginger and black beans. The sweetness of the salmon against the salty, faintly musty black beans is delicious, but the flavours stay subtle – there is no point in completely obliterating the delicacy of the fish.

---

sesame oil–water spray (see page 8)
6 oz (175 g) salmon fillet, skinned
juice of 1 lime
1 teaspoon teriyaki sauce
1 tablespoon medium dry sherry
¼ pint (150 ml) stock
pinch of sugar

1 garlic clove, crushed
slice of fresh root ginger, peeled and
 crushed
3 oz (75 g) Chinese leaves, shredded
1 tablespoon Chinese-style black bean
 sauce
freshly ground pepper, to taste

---

1. Heat a heavy-bottomed non-stick frying pan and spray with oil–water spray. Sear the salmon fillet on both sides until browned (just 1½ minutes in all). Set aside on a plate.

2. Mix the lime juice, teriyaki, sherry, stock and sugar together, and divide between two bowls. Add the garlic and ginger to one bowl, pour into the frying pan and cook, stirring, for 2–3 minutes, until the liquid is about gone.

3. Put the shredded cabbage into the pan with the remaining liquid, and stir-fry for 2–3 minutes, until the leaves have wilted. Stir in 1 tablespoon black bean sauce and a little freshly ground pepper.

4. Return the salmon fillet to the pan and heat to a simmer. Clap on a lid, remove from the heat, and let sit for 3–5 minutes, until just done. Put the stir-fried leaves on a plate with the salmon on top. Leave the juices in the pan and boil for approximately 1 minute to thicken. Pour and scrape the sauce over the salmon, and serve.

Oven-Poached Citrus Fish Fillets with Mango–Pepper Salsa

SERVES 2

ORANGE roughy is fished off New Zealand, and travels extremely well. I've seen it in major supermarket wet fish departments, as well as fishmongers. The fillets are thin, delicately flavoured, and cook in no time at all (less than 10 minutes). Here they are oven-poached in the Vinaigrette Base (in its pre-mustard stage, see page 23) and served with a sparkling fresh mango salsa. The recipe is easily doubled.

■

2 orange roughy fillets (about 6 oz/175 g each)
4 fl oz (110 ml) Vinaigrette Base (see page 23)
salt and freshly ground pepper, to taste

Salsa (Makes 1 pint/600 ml)
1 firm, ripe mango, peeled and diced (see page 10)
1 char-grilled red pepper, peeled (see page 9) and diced

½ chilli, deseeded and chopped
½ cucumber (about 6 oz/175 g), peeled, halved lengthwise, deseeded and diced
2 tablespoons chopped fresh coriander
2 tablespoons chopped fresh mint
salt and freshly ground pepper, to taste
2–3 tablespoons Vinaigrette Base (see page 23)

■

1. Preheat the oven to 220°C, 425°F, Gas Mark 7.

2. Combine the salsa ingredients and set aside.

3. Choose a shallow, glass baking dish that will hold the fillets in one uncrowded layer. Pour in the vinaigrette base. Turn the fish in the liquid, season with salt and pepper and put into the hot oven for 7 minutes.

4. Gently turn the fish (use a fish slice) and return to the oven for 2 minutes more if necessary. The fish should be moist, pearly, translucent, and just cooked. Don't overcook it, or you will ruin it. Gently transfer the fillets to a serving dish.

5. Pour the juices from the baking dish into a non-reactive frying pan, and boil quickly for about 1 minute, until reduced by about one third. Spoon some over the fish, spoon some salsa alongside each fillet, and serve. Serve the remaining pan juices in a small glass jug and the remaining salsa in a small bowl.

Monkfish with Red Wine Apricots

SERVES 2

MONKFISH is a huge, ugly beast – a real sea monster. The boned tail, blameless and featureless, is what you'll be taking home with you. It has a delicate taste and texture that is reminiscent of shellfish. It is absolutely imperative not to overcook monkfish, or it will become dry and fibrous. I was inspired to combine monkfish with wine-sautéed apricots (a brilliant combo) by a recipe in *Secret Ingredients*, an inspiring cookbook by talented American chef Michael Roberts.

---

olive oil–water spray (see page 8)
two 4 oz (110 g) pieces boneless, skinless
  monkfish
salt and freshly ground pepper, to taste
2 garlic cloves, crushed

9 fl oz (250 ml) red wine
9 fl oz (250 ml) stock
3 oz (75 g) ready-to-eat dried apricots,
  quartered
chopped fresh parsley, to serve

---

1. Preheat the oven to 220°C, 425°F, Gas Mark 7.

2. Spray a heavy-bottomed non-stick frying pan with oil–water spray. (Choose a pan that can go into the oven, and that will hold the monkfish in one uncrowded layer.) When smoking, brown the monkfish on all sides, turning with tongs (1½–2 minutes in all). Season with salt and pepper, and set aside on a plate.

3. Immediately add the garlic to the pan along with 2 fl oz (50 ml) wine and 2 fl oz (50 ml) stock. Boil down for about 1 minute, until the garlic is tender and in a syrupy glaze. Tip in the apricots and an additional 4 fl oz (100 ml) each of wine and stock, and simmer for 2–3 minutes. Add the monkfish tails and turn them in the mixture, then put the frying pan in the oven for 7 minutes. It is important not to overcook the fish; it should be juicy and pearly white, not fibrous and dry. Press it with your fingers; it should feel firm (not hard) and springy (not mushy).

4. Return the monkfish to the plate, and set the frying pan back on the hob. (Watch out for the pan handle – it's hot!) Pour the remaining wine and stock (3 fl oz/75 ml each) into the pan and boil for 2–3 minutes to reduce by half. Pour any juices that have collected under the monkfish into the pan.

5. Put the monkfish on a carving board, and slice into ½ inch (1 cm) medallions. Overlap on warm plates, and spoon some of the syrupy juices and apricots over them. Sprinkle with parsley and serve.

Variation

Monkfish in Garlic Red Wine Sauce

- Follow the recipe above, but omit the apricots. Increase the garlic to 4–6 large cloves.
- Spoon the garlic sauce over the finished medallions.

Sherried Fish Fillets with Glazed Mushrooms and Mango Sauce

SERVES 2–4

THIS is a wonderful combination of sherry-glazed fish, mango sauce (made with both fresh mango and mango chutney) and mushrooms sautéed in the low-fat mushroom 'trinity' of stock, sherry and teriyaki. Keep the components from swamping each other: arrange each fish fillet on a plate with a strip of sauce on one side, and a line of mushrooms on the other.

■

Fish

6 spring onions, trimmed and sliced

juice of 2 lemons

2 tablespoons medium dry sherry

2–4 white fish fillets (orange roughy, haddock, sole or plaice)

salt and freshly ground pepper, to taste

chopped fresh parsley

■

1. Combine the onions, lemon juice and sherry.

2. Arrange the fish fillets, in one uncrowded layer, in a non-reactive baking dish. Turn them to moisten, then leave, skin side up, to marinate for a few minutes.

3. Preheat the oven to 220°C, 425°F, Gas Mark 7.

4. Turn the fillets skin side down, season with salt and pepper, and bake in the oven for 7–10 minutes, until just done. Finally, sprinkle with chopped parsley.

■

Mango Sauce (Makes 1 pint/ 600 ml)

2 large onions, chopped

¾ pint (450 ml) stock

2 mangoes, peeled and diced (see page 10)

4 tablespoons mango chutney (use 2 tablespoons hot mango chutney and 2 tablespoons ordinary, if you like a bit of bite)

juice of 1 lime

grated rind of ½ lime

pinch of freshly grated nutmeg

salt and freshly ground pepper, to taste

■

1. Combine the onions and stock in a heavy-bottomed frying pan, cover, and boil for 5–7 minutes. Uncover, reduce the heat, and simmer for 3–5 minutes more, until the onions are tender.

2. Stir in the mango cubes, chutney, lime juice and rind, grated nutmeg, salt and pepper, and the remaining stock. Simmer for 7–10 minutes, until the mixture is thickened and savoury and the mango is cooked. Cool slightly, then purée in batches in a food processor or blender.

—— ∎ ——

Glazed Mushrooms (Makes 1 pint/600 ml)
1½ lb (675 g) small button mushrooms
2 fl oz (50 ml) stock
several dashes of teriyaki sauce
3 fl oz (75 ml) medium dry sherry
freshly ground pepper, to taste
salt (if needed)
additional sherry as needed

—— ∎ ——

1. Combine all the ingredients in a heavy-bottomed frying pan or wok. (Don't crowd the mushrooms into a small pan or they will steam rather than stir-fry.) Cook, stirring, over high heat for 7–10 minutes, until they exude quite a bit of liquid.

2. Continue to stir and cook for another 7–10 minutes, until the liquid has cooked down considerably. Reduce the heat a little, and cook until the mushrooms begin to stick and caramelise. Add a splash or two more of sherry, if necessary, and continue cooking until the mushrooms are beautifully glazed.

—— ∎ ——

To serve
chopped fresh coriander

—— ∎ ——

Put each fish fillet, sprinkled with juices from the baking dish, on a warmed plate. Spoon a strip of Mango Sauce alongside each fillet, and some mushrooms along the other side. Strew with fresh coriander, and serve.

Crumbed Grilled Plaice with Oriental Dipping Sauce

SERVES 2

A VERY elegant, Chinese-inspired low-fat stand-in for fried fish. Dabble each sesame- and ginger-scented bite in the dipping sauce before popping it into your mouth.

---

2 egg whites
1 tablespoon hoisin sauce
breadcrumbs for coating
1 teaspoon ground ginger
3 teaspoons sesame seeds
two 6 oz (175 g) plaice fillets
seasoned flour for coating
sesame oil–water spray (see page 8)

**Oriental Dipping Sauce
(Makes 4 fl oz/100 ml)**
juice of 1 orange
juice of ½ lime
juice of ½ lemon
1 garlic clove, crushed
½ inch (1 cm) piece fresh root ginger,
   peeled and crushed
several dashes of teriyaki sauce
2 teaspoons Chinese-style chilli sauce
   (to taste)

---

1. Preheat the grill to its highest temperature. Combine all the ingredients for the dipping sauce.

2. In a shallow soup plate, beat the egg whites lightly with the hoisin sauce. On a plate, combine the breadcrumbs with the ginger and sesame seeds.

3. Dredge the fillets in the seasoned flour, then dip in the egg white mixture. Finally, coat the flesh side of each fillet with breadcrumbs.

4. Spray the grill rack with oil–water spray and place the fillets on the rack, skin side down. Spray the fillets with oil–water spray, and grill 4 inches (10 cm) from the heat for approximately 5 minutes, until *just* done. The fish will be moist and translucent, and just beginning to flake. Serve with the dipping sauce.

Oven-Poached Cod with Oriental Basting Sauce

SERVES 2

COD CAN be very bland, especially when cooked without butter or oil. A fragrant marinade and a good dusting of sweet (Hungarian) paprika more than make up for the absence of fat.

———— • ————

2 pieces (12 oz/350 g) cod fillet
2 pinches of paprika
salt and freshly ground pepper, to taste
4 fl oz (100 ml) Oriental Dipping Sauce
  (see page 66)

2 fl oz (50 ml) stock
4 spring onions, trimmed and sliced

———— • ————

1. Preheat the oven to 220 °C, 425 °F, Gas Mark 7.

2. Rub the paprika into the fish fillets, and season with salt and pepper.

3. Combine the dipping sauce, stock and spring onions in an ovenproof dish. Roll the fish in the liquid and let it marinate while the oven preheats.

4. Put the fish into the hot oven, and bake for 10 minutes, until just done, basting with the pan juices halfway through.

Steamed Mussels

SERVES 2

A BIG bowlful of mussels and a loaf of good bread make a companionable, informal meal to share with a friend. Farmed mussels are available in net bags from fishmongers and supermarket wet fish departments. They couldn't be easier to prepare, and the pleasure of slurping each tender mussel from its shell, and mopping up the juices with rough hunks of crusty bread, can hardly be bettered. Serve 1 lb (450 g) mussels per person. Pull the first mussel out of its shell and eat it, then, for the rest, use that first pair of hinged shells as tweezers, to pluck the remaining mussels out of their shells. One of the great meals without a doubt!

---

2 lb (900 g) mussels
½ pint (300 ml) dry white wine or dry
   white vermouth
¼ pint (150 ml) water

1 large onion, finely chopped
4 spring onions, trimmed and sliced
2 tablespoons chopped fresh parsley
4 sprigs fresh thyme

---

1. Scrub the mussels to remove any grit and traces of barnacles, and pull and scrape away their wispy 'beards'. Discard any mussels that are cracked or abnormally heavy. Tap and squeeze any mussels that are not tightly closed; if they do not immediately close tightly, discard them. Swish the mussels around in a big bowl of cold water, drain, and repeat once more.

2. Combine the remaining ingredients in a deep, heavy saucepan that can be tightly covered. Bring to the boil.

3. Tip in the mussels and clap the cover on the pan. Simmer for 4–6 minutes, until they open. With oven gloves, pick up the pan halfway through, and give it a good shake. At the end of cooking, discard any mussels that have not opened.

4. Divide the mussels between two big bowls. Taste the mussel broth. If it seems gritty, strain it through a sieve lined with damp buttermuslin or two layers of coffee filter papers. Divide the broth between the two bowls. Have plenty of paper napkins on hand, and roll up your sleeves! (Place an extra bowl on the table for discarded shells.)

Variations

Instead of steaming the mussels in water and wine, use one of the tomato sauces (with plenty of chilli, garlic and fresh herbs, and thinned a bit with broth) in the sauce or pasta chapters (see pages 28–29 and 46).

Prawn, Mango and Fennel Salad

MAKES 1½ PINTS (900 ml)

THIS is a vivid and exciting salad to serve as a stunning first course, or a light summer lunch or supper dish. The crisp anise of the fennel against the sweet juiciness of the orange and mango; the sharp bite of the chilli, the peppery leafiness of the rocket, the suave mustard-scented smoky dressing (not to mention the glorious colours) provide an enormously pleasurable sensory experience. *This* is what quick cooking and eating is all about: chop it all up, throw it together, wallow in its glory.

———— ■ ————

Mango and Pepper 'Mayo' (see page 27)
rocket, watercress and lamb's lettuce, to serve
8 oz (225 g) tiny cooked, peeled prawns
fresh mint leaves, torn into strips

Salad
1 orange, peeled and diced
1 firm ripe mango, peeled and diced (see page 10)

1 bulb fennel, trimmed and diced
1 yellow (or green) courgette, diced
½ chilli, deseeded and diced (or more to taste)
1 tablespoon chopped fresh mint
1 tablespoon chopped fresh parsley
4 tablespoons orange juice
2 tablespoons lime juice
salt and freshly ground pepper, to taste

———— ■ ————

1. Toss together the salad ingredients, and then fold in half of the mango dressing.

2. Arrange on a bed of rocket, watercress and lamb's lettuce. Sprinkle the prawns on top and strew on strips of fresh mint. Serve the remainder of the dressing separately.

Prawn Cocktail with a Difference

PRAWN cocktail is out of favour – one of the dodos of gastronomy. What a pity: perfectly steamed prawns with a nice, spicy dunking sauce (lots of prawns, lots of sauce, a heap of peppery greens) make an indulgently luxurious, informal fast meal. The idea is to eat the prawns one by one with your fingers, dabbling each one enthusiastically into the sauce as you go. Serve the prawns on a bed of greens (herb salad or rocket, lamb's lettuce, etc.) with a generous ramekin of sauce for dipping. Some halved or quartered 'flavour' tomatoes, and a few draped strips of grilled pepper certainly wouldn't hurt. Make the sauce a feisty one: try Mango and Pepper 'Mayo' (see page 27); Chilli Sauce (see page 15) or the Spicy Cocktail Sauce below.

To Steam Prawns

Rinse peeled, deveined (see page 49) tiger prawns under cold running water. Lay the wet prawns in one layer in a heavy-bottomed non-stick pan. Put the lid on the pan, turn the heat to high, and steam for 3–4 minutes (stir them once, halfway through) until *just* done (they will turn pink and begin to curl). *Immediately* spread the prawns on a cold plate, and put the plate on a rack to cool slightly. Don't chill them – eat them at once, when they are at their juicy best.

Spicy Cocktail Sauce

MAKES APPROXIMATELY ½ PINT (300 ml)

———— • ————

½ pint (300 ml) tomato ketchup
several dashes of Tabasco sauce
several dashes of Worcestershire sauce

½ tablespoon hot mango chutney or
   Chinese-style chilli sauce
chopped fresh herbs (e.g. flat-leaf
   parsley, coriander)

———— • ————

Combine the ingredients in a blender, and blend to a rough purée.

Rosemary Prawns

MAKES 1 PINT (600 ml)

A MEDITERRANEAN treatment for prawns, with a few slivered black olives standing in for the extra-virgin olive oil. If you can't find fish stock, use chicken or vegetable.

———— ▪ ————

3 dry-pack sundried tomatoes, chopped (use scissors)

3 black olives in brine, drained and slivered off their stones

2 garlic cloves, crushed

2 tablespoons chopped fresh rosemary leaves, or 1 tablespoon dried rosemary

2 fl oz (50 ml) medium dry sherry

4 fl oz (100 ml) fish stock

several dashes of Worcestershire sauce

several dashes of Tabasco sauce

2 tablespoons lemon juice

salt and freshly ground pepper, to taste

olive oil–water spray (see page 8)

1 lb (450 g) tiger prawns, peeled and deveined (see page 49)

chopped fresh parsley, to garnish

———— ▪ ————

1. Combine all the ingredients, except the oil spray, prawns and garnish.

2. Spray a non-stick wok with olive oil–water spray and heat. Tip in the prawns, and stir-fry for 1–2 minutes, until the prawns are half cooked. Transfer to a plate.

3. Pour the herb–stock mixture into the wok, and boil down for 3–5 minutes, until half its volume. Tip in the prawns, and stir-fry for 1½–2 minutes, until just done. Do not overcook. Sprinkle with parsley and serve hot with rice, couscous or plenty of crusty bread, or cool, surrounded by quartered small 'flavour' tomatoes and wedges of fresh peaches (in season).

Smoky Fish Cakes

MAKES 11–12

I ENJOY taking a familiar and homely everyday recipe, shaking it up a bit, and giving it a spicy ethnic twist. It makes life so much more interesting. Here, good old fish and mashed potato cakes get the treatment. I think you will find that everyone eats at least three. Serve these crusty beauties with a splendid cold sauce: Rémoulade (see page 29), Chilli (see page 15) or Spicy Cocktail Sauce (see page 70).

■

9 fl oz (250 ml) well-seasoned stock

2 oz (50 g) mashed potato flakes (e.g. Mr Mash)

approximately 8 tablespoons flour

3 egg whites

approximately 10 tablespoons bread-crumbs, seasoned with salt, pepper and a touch of cayenne

7½ oz (213 g) can red salmon, drained and flaked (discard any skin)

5 oz (150 g) smoked trout, flaked

3 spring onions, trimmed and sliced

½ inch (1 cm) piece fresh root ginger, peeled and crushed

4 tablespoons roughly chopped fresh coriander

1 tablespoon chopped fresh parsley

several dashes of Tabasco sauce

several dashes of Worcestershire sauce

2 tablespoons hot mango chutney

juice of 1 lime

oil–water spray (see page 8)

■

1. Bring the stock to the boil in a saucepan, remove from the heat and mix in the potato flakes. Spread out the mashed potato on a plate and put in the freezer to cool.

2. Preheat the grill to high.

3. Spread the flour on a plate, put two of the egg whites in a shallow bowl and beat lightly, and spread the seasoned crumbs on another plate.

4. Put the fish, remaining egg white, spring onions, ginger, coriander, parsley, Tabasco and Worcestershire sauces, chutney and lime juice in a food processor. Add the cooled potato mixture and process to a rough purée. Form into 11–12 cakes.

5. Dredge the fish cakes in flour, then egg white, then crumbs, coating them thoroughly. Spray the grill rack with oil–water spray, place the fish cakes on the rack, and spray with oil–water spray. Grill approximately 4 inches (10 cm) from the heat for 3–5 minutes on each side (spraying them again when you have turned them), until golden and puffed.

TAKE A CAN OF TUNA

Fresh tuna flesh is red and meaty – almost like very fine, juicy (if not over-cooked) steak. Canned tuna is quite different – a thing (a very *good* thing!) unto itself. A stack of tuna cans in the cupboard is a must for hurried cooks. Canned tuna is an amiable product and will enthusiastically combine with many different ethnic flavours.

Tuna Bean Salad

MAKES 1½ PINTS (900 ml); SERVES 2–3

THIS is a reworking of a classic Italian recipe – all that's missing is the lashings of olive oil. For an even quicker version, toss the tuna, beans and herbs with several tablespoons of White Bean and Olive Vinaigrette (see page 24). Use two tablespoons of the cannellini beans to make the vinaigrette, and the remainder in the salad. Either way, the salad is delicious served on a bed of greens, surrounded by halved cherry tomatoes and garnished with shredded basil.

•

10 spring onions, trimmed and thinly sliced
4 black olives in brine, drained and slivered off their stones
4 dry-pack sundried tomatoes, diced (use scissors), optional
1 garlic clove, crushed
pinch of crushed dried chillies
½ pint (300 ml) stock

7 oz (200 g) can tuna in brine, drained
14 oz (400 g) can cannellini beans, drained
2 tablespoons balsamic vinegar
1 tablespoon drained capers, chopped
½ tablespoon lemon juice
1–2 tablespoons shredded fresh basil
1 tablespoon chopped fresh parsley

•

1. Combine the onions, olives, sundried tomatoes, garlic, chilli and stock in a non-reactive frying pan, cover and boil for 5–7 minutes. Uncover and simmer for 3–4 minutes, until the onions are tender and the liquid is almost gone.

2. Combine with the remaining ingredients and mix thoroughly.

Tuna and Vegetables in a Chinese Dressing

MAKES ¾ PINT (450 ml); SERVES 2

THE PREVIOUS recipe is a reworking of a classic Italian combination; here the tuna mixes happily with Chinese flavourings. Serve the salad on a bed of dark green leaves (spinach or watercress, for instance) surrounded by Oriental Beetroot Salad (see page 120). Sprinkle with some chopped fresh coriander, if you like it.

—— • ——

2 garlic cloves, crushed
½ inch (1 cm) slice fresh root ginger,
  peeled and crushed
4 tablespoons wine vinegar
several dashes of Tabasco sauce
2 teaspoons Chinese-style black bean
  sauce
1 tablespoon hoisin sauce

1 tablespoon runny honey
7 oz (200 g) can tuna in brine, drained
2 small carrots, grated
6 spring onions, trimmed and thinly
  sliced
2 small inner stalks of celery with leaves,
  diced
salt and freshly ground pepper, to taste

—— • ——

1. In a small bowl, combine the garlic, ginger, vinegar, Tabasco, black bean sauce, hoisin and honey. Leave to marinate for a few minutes.

2. Flake the tuna into a bowl, and mix in the vegetables. Mix in the dressing and season with salt and pepper.

· CHAPTER 5 ·

Poultry

CHICKENS and ducks have plenty of fat in and under the skin; poultry becomes low-fat food only when that skin and fat have been totally removed. Poultry fat has scads of flavour, so fat removal can also mean that the poultry becomes terribly boring and bland (I should say even blander than it already is in these days of mass production). Remedy this by using lively seasonings, and cooking the poultry in ways that infuse the flesh with plenty of flavour. For quick cookery, parts cook faster than whole birds. I particularly like chicken thighs (much more flavour than the bland breasts), quartered poussins, and duck breasts. It's not an option to cook them quickly – it's an imperative. Like fish, they are totally spoiled by overcooking – overcooked poultry is tough, dry and stringy.

Thai-Style Chicken Noodle Salad

MAKES 2 PINTS (1.1 litres); SERVES 2–4

A RIDGED 'grill' pan, designed for the hob, gives boneless chicken breasts a wonderfully smoky barbecued taste. As it cooks, brush with some of the dressing so that the chicken takes on a spicy sticky glaze. The glaze, and the barbecue smokiness, give the chicken quite a lot of character. Cook the chicken until it is *just* done so that the texture is creamy rather than stringy.

•

2–4 skinless, boneless chicken breasts
sesame oil – water spray (see page 8)
½ package (3 oz/75 g) Chinese egg
   thread noodles, broken into three
1 small carrot, peeled
½ cucumber, peeled, halved lengthwise
   and deseeded
4 spring onions, trimmed
2 tablespoons shredded fresh mint
2 tablespoons chopped fresh coriander

Spicy Thai Dressing
1 tablespoon Thai fish sauce
2 tablespoons Worcestershire sauce
2 tablespoons Chinese-style chilli sauce
1 tablespoon sugar
2 garlic cloves, crushed
1 inch (2.5 cm) piece fresh root
   ginger, peeled and crushed

•

1. Put the kettle on to boil. Meanwhile combine all the dressing ingredients. Put 1 tablespoon of the dressing on a plate, and set the rest aside.

2. Dredge the chicken breasts in the tablespoon of dressing. Spray a ridged 'grill' pan (for use on the hob) with oil–water spray and heat. Sear the chicken for 1–2 minutes on each side so that it is well striped with grill marks. Brush it with the dressing and spray with oil–water spray as you turn it. Turn the heat down a little, and let cook, turning and brushing, for another 2 minutes. Clap on a lid, remove from the heat and let sit while you complete the preparation.

3. Put the noodles in a bowl and pour the boiling water over them. Let sit for 3–4 minutes, until just cooked.

4. Grate the carrot, chop the cucumber and slice the spring onions.

5. Drain the noodles and put them in a bowl. Add the remaining dressing and mix well. Mix in the vegetables, then spread the mixture on a platter.

6. The chicken is done when it feels firm yet springy. Slice it crossways. Place the sliced breasts on the noodles and vegetables, sprinkle with herbs and serve.

Chicken with Porcini Mushrooms

MAKES 4 PIECES

SKINNED chicken thighs become perfectly browned and glazed if they are first braised in liquid in a non-stick pan, then allowed to brown slowly. In this recipe, the chicken braises in stock and wine with dried *porcini* (cep) mushrooms. The mushrooms are not reconstituted first – they reconstitute as they braise. Rinse them in cold water before use and choose flat pieces that are not likely to have grit-filled nooks and crannies.

—— ▪ ——

4 chicken thighs (bone in), skinned and trimmed of skin, fat and gristle
2–3 fresh sage leaves, torn in half
1–2 sprigs fresh rosemary
1 oz (25 g) dried porcini (cep)

mushrooms, rinsed and cut into small pieces (use scissors)
salt and freshly ground pepper, to taste
8 fl oz (225 ml) stock
8 fl oz (225 ml) dry white wine

—— ▪ ——

1. Put the chicken thighs, skinned side down, into a heavy bottomed, non-reactive frying pan or shallow flameproof casserole. Scatter in the herbs and the mushroom pieces, and sprinkle with salt and pepper. Pour in 5 fl oz (150 ml) stock and 5 fl oz (150 ml) wine, and bring to a simmer.

2. Simmer, uncovered, for 10–13 minutes, turning the chicken with tongs every few minutes, until the chicken is about half done. Pour approximately half the pan liquid into a measuring jug or bowl and set aside.

3. Continue simmering the chicken, turning it occasionally, for a further 10–15 minutes, until the liquid remaining in the pan is very thick and reduced, and the chicken is almost cooked through. (If the liquid is *not* thick and reduced, remove the chicken to a plate and cover loosely with foil to keep it warm. Boil down the pan juices until they *are* thickened and reduced. Return the chicken to the pan.)

4. Turn the heat up a little and cook, turning the chicken frequently, until the pieces are just cooked through, and richly glazed. Put the chicken on a plate and cover loosely with foil.

5. Pour the remaining wine and stock into the pan, bring to the boil, and boil, scraping up the browned bits, for 2–3 minutes, until reduced almost to a glaze. Pour in the reserved pan liquid. Boil for 2–3 minutes until very thick, reduced and concentrated. Return the chicken to the pan and turn in the sauce to heat through. Serve at once.

Pan-Braised Chicken with Garlic

MAKES 4 PIECES

THIS is a quick, lower-fat variation of a classic dish. Don't be frightened of using 20 cloves of garlic; the cloves caramelise and turn fabulously soft and sweet. If you use the sweeter vermouth bianco (with a little added lemon juice) instead of dry white vermouth, the garlic will caramelise even more, and the chicken will have a pronounced sweet and sour flavour. Serve the dish with plenty of crusty bread to mop up the juices, and on which to spread the voluptuous garlic.

•

4 chicken thighs (bone in), skinned and
well trimmed
4 fl oz (100 ml) stock, plus more if
needed
4 fl oz (100 ml) dry white vermouth, or
4 fl oz (100 ml) vermouth bianco and
the juice of 1 lemon, plus more if
needed

20 garlic cloves, sliced in half lengthwise
1 teaspoon dried tarragon, crumbled
salt and freshly ground pepper, to taste

•

1. Arrange the chicken, skinned side down, in a heavy-bottomed frying pan (large enough for the chicken to be in one uncrowded layer). Pour in the liquid, and scatter the garlic and tarragon around the chicken. Season with salt and pepper, and bring to a simmer.

2. Cook, uncovered, turning the chicken occasionally, for about 20 minutes. As it cooks, the liquid will cook down considerably and the garlic will almost melt. Once the juices have become thick and syrupy, the chicken will brown nicely (turn it frequently at this point). When the chicken is tender, there is no pink at the bone, and the garlic is very tender and almost caramelised, in a thick syrupy sauce, the dish is done.

3. If, during cooking, the liquid cooks away, add a little more, as needed. If, on the other hand, the chicken is tender and cooked through, and there is a considerable amount of liquid left, remove the chicken and garlic to a plate, and boil the pan juices down, then return the chicken to the sauce.

Chicken in Spicy Mushroom Gravy

MAKES 4 PIECES

CHICKEN thigh fillets (skinned *and* boned) cook very quickly indeed – almost as quickly as breast fillets – but the flavour is much more robust than the bland breasts. Thigh fillets, ready boned and skinned, are now available in most supermarkets, but they tend to be rather raggedy, and they will need to be trimmed of all their fat. If you can't find them, it is a simple matter to bone and skin chicken thighs yourself.

———— **.** ————

1 tablespoon each of ground coriander, cumin and paprika
½ teaspoon mild chilli powder
4 chicken thigh fillets, well trimmed
salt and freshly ground pepper, to taste
olive oil–water spray (see page 8)
approximately ¼ pint (150 ml) chicken stock

4 fl oz (100 ml) dry white wine
8 oz (225 g) mushrooms, sliced
dash or two of teriyaki sauce
1 tablespoon tomato purée
1 teaspoon Dijon mustard
several dashes of Tabasco sauce
a few drops of lemon juice
chopped fresh parsley, to garnish

———— **.** ————

1. Combine the spices, and spread them on a plate. Dredge the chicken pieces in the mixture until they are very well coated on both sides. Season with salt and pepper on both sides.

2. Spray a heavy-bottomed frying pan with oil–water spray. (The pan should be of a size to hold the chicken in one uncrowded layer.) Sear the chicken on both sides, turning with tongs, for 1–2 minutes. Pour in approximately 2 fl oz (50 ml) of the stock and 1 fl oz (25 ml) of the wine. It will bubble furiously. Turn the chicken in the liquid, over high heat, until just cooked through and glazed (5–7 minutes in all). Add more stock and wine, as needed. Put the chicken on a plate.

3. Tip the mushrooms into the frying pan. Add 2 fl oz (50 ml) each of the remaining stock and wine, the teriyaki sauce and a bit of salt and pepper. Stir and cook for about 5 minutes, until the mushrooms are tender.

4. Stir in the tomato purée, Dijon mustard, Tabasco sauce and lemon juice. Simmer for 2–3 minutes to thicken, and to blend the flavours. Add the chicken to the mushrooms and turn to heat through. Put the chicken on a serving dish and heap on the mushroom sauce. (Use a rubber spatula to scrape out every last bit.) Sprinkle with parsley and serve.

Glazed Orange Chicken

MAKES 4 PIECES

SWEET and sour, with a subtle hint of curry – perfect served with Golden Spice Pan-Roasted Potatoes (see page 117) and watercress.

— • —

4 chicken thigh fillets, skinned and well
  trimmed
2 tablespoons runny honey
grated rind of ½ orange
grated rind of ½ lime
juice of 1 lemon (about 2 fl oz/50 ml)
1 teaspoon Dijon mustard

½ teaspoon mild korma curry powder
½ inch (1 cm) piece fresh root ginger,
  peeled and crushed
1 lemon, halved and deseeded
chopped fresh parsley and coriander, to
  garnish

— • —

1. Put the chicken thighs in a frying pan that will hold them in one uncrowded layer.

2. Whisk together all the remaining ingredients, except the halved lemon and the herb garnish, and pour over the chicken. Turn the chicken several times in the honey–mustard mixture, then cook over high heat, turning constantly, for 7–10 minutes, until just done and coated in the glaze.

3. Towards the end of the cooking time, as the greatly reduced and thickened sauce begins to catch, squeeze in more lemon juice and scrape the browned bits from the bottom of the pan as you stir and turn the chicken pieces. To serve, sprinkle with herbs.

Chicken in Creamy Spinach Sauce

4 PIECES

I'VE ALWAYS loved the flavour principles of Hungarian cookery, but lard, goose fat and soured cream make it problematical (to put it mildly) for low-fat foodies. Fortunately, the distinctive spices of Hungarian cuisine transfer nicely to lower-fat variations. Use caraway and paprika to coat thigh fillets, then make a quick piquant and creamy green-flecked sauce with ricotta, fresh spinach and good old Dijon.

•

2 tablespoons paprika
½ teaspoon ground white pepper
½ teaspoon caraway seeds (optional)
4 chicken thigh fillets, skinned and well
   trimmed
salt, to taste
oil–water spray (see page 8)
approximately 4 fl oz (100 ml) stock

4 fl oz (100 ml) dry white wine
pinch of sugar
8 oz (225 g) baby spinach leaves, washed
2 generous tablespoons ricotta cheese
1 teaspoon Dijon mustard
several dashes of Tabasco sauce
   (optional)

•

1. Mix the paprika, pepper and caraway seeds, if using, and spread on a plate. Dredge the chicken pieces in the spices, and season with salt.

2. Spray a heavy-bottomed frying pan with oil–water spray (the pan should hold the chicken in one uncrowded layer) and heat. Sear the chicken pieces on both sides (about 1½ minutes in all), then pour in 2 fl oz (50 ml) each of the stock and wine, and add a pinch of sugar. It will bubble furiously. Keep the heat high as you turn the chicken in the liquid until it is just done (5–7 minutes). Transfer the chicken to a plate.

3. Add about another 1 fl oz (25 ml) each of the stock and wine, and stir in the spinach. Season with salt. Stir and cook for a minute or so, until the spinach is just cooked but still bright green. Scrape the contents of the pan into a food processor. Add the ricotta and mustard (and Tabasco if you want a bit of bite), and process until very finely chopped.

4. Tip the mixture back into the pan, add any juices rendered from the waiting chicken pieces, and simmer gently for about 1 minute. Turn the chicken pieces in the sauce to warm through. Put the chicken fillets on a serving plate, pour the sauce over and around them, and serve at once.

Chicken Thighs Braised in Mango Vinaigrette with Peach and Mango Chutney

MAKES 4 PIECES

THE MANGO Chutney Vinaigrette on page 26 makes a dynamite marinade for thigh fillets. When the fillets are done, the marinade is cooked down into a rich, dark, powerful sauce. Serve with watercress or lamb's lettuce, on the same plate. A few potatoes wouldn't hurt either.

•

4 chicken thigh fillets, skinned and well trimmed
salt and freshly ground pepper, to taste
Mango Chutney Vinaigrette (see page 26)
oil–water spray (see page 8)

Chutney (Makes approximately ½ pint/300 ml)
1 firm, ripe peach, stoned and diced
1 ripe mango, peeled, and diced (see page 10)
1 tablespoon chopped fresh coriander
1–1½ teaspoons chilli sauce
1 tablespoon Mango Chutney Vinaigrette (see page 26)

•

1. Combine all the chutney ingredients and refrigerate until needed.

2. Put the chicken into a baking dish, season with salt and pepper, and toss well with 4 fl oz (100 ml) of the vinaigrette. Let marinate for 20–30 minutes, if possible, although 5–10 minutes will do, if you are pressed.

3. Spray a heavy-bottomed frying pan (choose one that can hold the chicken pieces in one uncrowded layer) with oil–water spray, and heat it. Take the thighs out of the marinade, and sear in the pan, on both sides (1–2 minutes in all). Pour in half the marinade, reduce the heat slightly, and simmer, turning frequently, for 5–7 minutes, until the chicken is just done, glazed, and coated in a scant, rich sauce. Put the chicken on a plate and scrape the pan juices over it.

4. Pour the rest of the marinade, plus 2–3 fl oz (50–75 ml) additional vinaigrette, into the pan and boil down by about half until thickened and dark. Return the chicken to the pan and turn in the sauce to heat through. Serve at once, accompanied by the peach and mango chutney.

Roasted Poussins

MAKES 8 PIECES

POUSSINS — adorable little mini-birds — are a quick way to give yourself a chicken dinner. Quarter them (easily done with kitchen scissors), rub a savoury mixture under the skin (these darlings can be bland) and roast in a hot oven. A single poussin will feed one or two, depending on appetite and accompaniments.

---

4 garlic cloves

2 black olives in brine, drained and slivered off their stones

1 inch (2.5 cm) piece fresh root ginger, peeled

1 teaspoon ground cumin

½ teaspoon ground coriander

¼ teaspoon ground cinnamon

pinch or two of ground cayenne

juice of ½ lime

8 fl oz (225 ml) stock

2 poussins (approximately 14 oz/400 g each), quartered (see Note below)

salt and freshly ground pepper, to taste

additional ground cumin and paprika, to taste

---

1. Preheat the oven to 230°C, 450°F, Gas Mark 8.

2. Crush together the garlic, olives and ginger (use a pestle and mortar, a kitchen mallet, or the side of a knife blade). Combine in a small frying pan with the spices, lime juice and stock, and simmer for 5–7 minutes, until the liquid is about gone. Cool slightly.

3. Loosen the skin on the poussin quarters. Push and rub the spice mixture under the skin. Season with salt and pepper, cumin and paprika. Spray a baking sheet with oil–water spray, and arrange the quarters, skin side down, on the tray. Roast in the oven for 15 minutes, then turn and roast, skin side up, for 15 minutes, until the juices run clear. Serve on a bed of rocket or herb salad surrounded by Pan-Roasted Potatoes (see page 116).

Note

To quarter a poussin, use your kitchen scissors to cut on either side of the backbone. Discard the backbone. Flip over and cut in two through the breastbone. Halve each half by cutting between the leg and the wing.

Grilled Duck Breasts with Sour Cherry and Red Onion Chutney

SERVES 2–4

A WHOLE duck, when roasted, simply weeps fat – trying to defat it for a low-fat regime is just too tedious and thankless. But breast fillets (available in packs of two from many supermarkets) are easy. Simply strip off the skin with all its attendant fat (just pull, using a knife to ease it along), and pan-fry or grill the breast (now lean as can be) in an oil-sprayed non-stick frying pan or ridged 'grill' pan. The flesh is rich and red – almost like fine steak, and is best served pink (slightly rare). A tart and spicy fresh chutney based on dried sour cherries sets it off brilliantly.

———— ▪ ————

2–4 duck breast fillets, skinned
salt and freshly ground pepper, to taste
oil–water spray (see page 8)
1–2 tablespoons chopped fresh coriander
1–2 tablespoons chopped fresh parsley

Chutney (Makes 12 fl oz/350 ml)
½ red chilli, deseeded and chopped
½ green chilli, deseeded and chopped
2 garlic cloves, crushed
1 inch (2.5 cm) piece fresh root ginger,
   peeled and crushed
3 dry-pack sundried tomatoes, roughly
   chopped (use scissors)

1 large red onion, very roughly chopped
4 fl oz (100 ml) red wine
½ pint (300 ml) stock
juice of ½ lime, lemon and orange
1 tablespoon Worcestershire sauce
several dashes of teriyaki sauce
several dashes of Tabasco sauce
1 tablespoon balsamic vinegar
3 oz (75 g) dried sour cherries
1 teaspoon ground cumin
½ teaspoon ground coriander
pinch of sugar

———— ▪ ————

1. Combine all the chutney ingredients in a heavy-bottomed or non-stick frying pan, and simmer for 10–15 minutes, until thick and syrupy. Taste and add a little more lemon juice or sugar, as needed, to give a nice balance of sweet and sour. Leave in the pan.

2. Sprinkle the duck breasts with salt and a generous amount of freshly ground pepper. Spray a ridged 'grill' pan (for use on the hob) with oil–water spray, and heat. Sear the duck breasts on both sides, then reduce the heat a little and cook for approximately 3 minutes on each side. The duck should remain quite rare inside.

3. Add the duck breasts to the chutney. Simmer, turning the duck in the pan, until it is nicely glazed (3–4 minutes) and cooked the way you like it. (For best results, it should remain pink inside. It will feel firm yet springy when pressed with your finger.)

4. Put the duck on a board and slice crossways on the diagonal. Put a few spoonfuls of the chutney on a warm plate, arrange the slices on the chutney, and scrape on any juices from the board. Sprinkle with herbs and serve.

Chinese Duck Breasts in Pancakes

SERVES 2

OCCASIONALLY see Chinese pancakes in chill cabinets of various super-markets. If you can't find them, commit ethnic heresy by serving this lean and quick version of Peking duck in Mexican wheat tortillas, which are widely available. In these post-modern times, why not? I've resorted to the tortilla option several times, and can report that it works very well indeed.

•

2 duck breast fillets, skinned
salt and freshly ground pepper, to taste
sesame oil–water spray (see page 8)

Pan Sauce
1 garlic clove, crushed
½ inch (1 cm) piece fresh root ginger,
   peeled and crushed
3 spring onions, trimmed and sliced
juice of ½ orange
½ teaspoon Thai fish sauce
½ teaspoon teriyaki sauce
1 teaspoon Chinese black bean sauce
½ teaspoon Chinese-style chilli sauce
4 fl oz (100 ml) stock, plus an additional
   1 fl oz (25 ml) if needed

To Serve
1 package Chinese pancakes, steamed
   according to package directions, or a
   package of wheat tortillas, wrapped in
   foil and heated in a hot oven for 3–5
   minutes
½ cucumber, peeled, deseeded and
   slivered lengthways
4 spring onions, white part only trimmed,
   slivered lengthways
chopped fresh coriander
hoisin sauce

•

1. Combine all the sauce ingredients in a shallow bowl.

2. Season the duck breasts lightly with salt and pepper. Pierce them in several places with a thin skewer, such as a cake tester, then dredge them well in the sauce. Leave them in the sauce while you spray a ridged 'grill' pan (for use on the hob) with oil–water spray, and heat until very hot.

3. Put the duck into the pan (leaving the sauce in the bowl) and sear on both sides, spraying with oil–water as you turn them (2–3 minutes in all). When the duck breasts are well striped with griddle marks; reduce the heat a little and cook, turning occasionally, for about 3 minutes on each side. The duck should remain quite rare.

4. Put the sauce into a small frying pan that will hold the duck in one layer, and bring to the boil. Transfer the duck to the sauce and reduce to a

simmer. Add 1 fl oz (25 ml) more stock if it is cooking down too rapidly. Simmer, turning the duck in the sauce for 3–4 minutes until it is coated in a syrupy glaze, and cooked the way you like it. (For best results the duck should remain pink inside; it will feel firm yet springy.) Set aside to rest, while you set out the pancakes, the slivered vegetables, the chopped coriander and the hoisin sauce.

5. Carve the duck crossways and set on a platter. To eat, spread some hoisin sauce on a pancake, sprinkle on some vegetables and coriander, and top with a few slices of duck and sauce. Roll up like a taco, and bite into it. Juicy, smoky, spicy . . . sheer heaven.

Duck Fajitas

SERVES 2

FAJITAS (pronounced fa-*hee*-tas) started out as rough cowboy food – strips of grilled skirt steak and chillies wrapped in tortillas and gnawed on the hoof, as it were. Now they seem to pop up everywhere, from wine bars to pubs, in all sorts of interesting guises, from vegetarian to prawn to chicken. Duck breast, with its red, deeply steak-like character, seems the perfect low-fat choice for a he-man's (and she-woman's) fajita. Dredge it in spices, adorn it with a spicy citrus sauce, lavish it with charred vegetables, wrap it tenderly in a warm tortilla, and you will find yourself in cow person's heaven.

—— ∎ ——

2 duck breast fillets, skinned
1 teaspoon each of ground coriander,
   ground paprika and ground cumin,
   mixed and spread on a plate
salt and freshly ground pepper, to taste
olive oil–water spray (see page 8)

Pan Sauce

juice of 1 lime
juice of ½ orange
1 dry-pack sundried tomato, chopped
   (use scissors)
½–1 chilli, deseeded and chopped
1 garlic clove, crushed
pinch of sugar
3 spring onions, trimmed and chopped

2 black olives in brine, drained and
   slivered off their stones
2 fl oz (50 ml) chicken stock, plus extra if
   needed

Vegetables

1 small courgette, trimmed and sliced
   lengthwise, and each slice quartered
½ red onion, sliced into thin half circles
   and the pieces separated
char-grilled peppers (see page 9),
   optional

To Serve

wheat tortillas
Simple Tomato Salsa (see page 19)

—— ∎ ——

1. Pierce the duck breasts in several places with a thin skewer (such as a cake tester), and dredge in the spice mix. Season with salt and pepper, and set aside.

2. Combine the sauce ingredients in a small frying pan that will hold the duck breasts in one layer. Bring to the boil.

3. Spray a ridged 'grill' pan (for use on the hob) with olive oil–water spray, and heat. Sear the duck breasts on both sides in the grill pan, spraying with oil–water spray as you turn them, until they are well striped with griddle marks (2–3 minutes in all). Reduce the heat a little and cook the

duck breasts, turning occasionally, for about 3 minutes on each side. The duck should remain quite rare.

4. Transfer the duck to the sauce and reduce to a simmer. Add a little more stock, if it has cooked down too rapidly. Simmer, turning the duck in the sauce, for 3–4 minutes, until it is in a syrupy glaze, and cooked the way you like it. (For best results, the duck should remain pink inside; it will feel firm yet springy.) Set aside to rest.

5. Spray the 'grill' pan again with oil–water spray, turn up the heat, and throw in the courgette and red onion. Stir, spraying with oil–water spray once or twice, until tender and speckled with charred bits.

6. Slice the duck breasts crossways and put on a platter. Surround with the grilled vegetables. One at a time, heat the tortillas in the 'grill' pan for just a few seconds on each side. (Don't oil spray them.) They should stay pliable; if you grill them for too long they will turn crisp. To eat, put some duck, with its juices, on a tortilla. Top with vegetables, add some salsa, wrap and eat joyfully.

Pan-Braised Poussin with Figs

MAKES 4 PIECES

LIKE chicken thighs, poussin quarters benefit from pan-braising. Lively seasonings counteract their tendency towards blandness. The intriguing combination of dried figs, chillies and garlic, braised, with the poussins, in balsamic vinegar, Worcestershire sauce and lime, gives the finished dish a dark and spicy dimension.

---

1 poussin, quartered (see page 83)
salt and freshly ground pepper, to taste
4 ready-to-eat dried figs, stemmed and
  quartered
2 garlic cloves, crushed
1 large chilli, deseeded and chopped
½ teaspoon paprika

1 tablespoon balsamic vinegar
1 tablespoon Worcestershire sauce
¼–½ tablespoon Tabasco sauce
juice of 1 lime
5–8 fl oz (150–225 ml) stock
1–2 tablespoons chopped fresh parsley
1–2 tablespoons chopped fresh coriander

---

1. Pull all the skin off the poussin quarters. Sprinkle with salt and pepper, and set aside.

2. Choose a non-stick or heavy-bottomed frying pan that will comfortably hold the poussin pieces in one layer. Stir all the remaining ingredients, except the stock and herbs, into the pan. Stir in approximately 5 fl oz (150 ml) stock, and add the poussin pieces, skinned side down.

3. Simmer, uncovered, turning the pieces occasionally, for 15–20 minutes, until the chicken is richly glazed and just done (the juices will run clear, and there will be no trace of pink at the bone). The breast portions are likely to be done first – remove them from the pan and cover loosely, then return to the pan at the last minute. Add more stock as needed.

4. Taste and adjust the seasoning if necessary. To serve, sprinkle with the fresh herbs.

OPPOSITE Monkfish with Red-Wine Apricots (page 62) served with Pan-Braised Fennel (page 112) and mashed potato with added chopped herbs

· CHAPTER 6 ·

Meat

UNLESS you are a determined vegetarian, there is no need to give up meat in the name of a low-fat diet. Simply give up *fatty* meat. Red meat is a rich source of important nutrients (iron, zinc, B vitamins); a few (lean) meat meals each week will enhance your general nutritional profile. And remember: although *not* vegetarian, meat dishes should be intermingled with and surrounded by oodles of glorious vegetables. Plenty of vegetables, a good measure of fruit and grains, with a generous amount of fish, a bit of lean poultry and lean meat here and there, all combine to make an exemplary low-fat, highly nutritious – and highly delicious – culinary way of life.

OPPOSITE Wine-Glazed Pan-Fried Burgers (page 93) topped with Roasted Tomato Swirl (page 17) and accompanied by Black-Eyed Bean and Corn Salad (page 105)

Citrus-Scented Burgers

MAKES 4–6 (1–2 burgers make a good serving)

BURGERS have been degraded. These days, the word conjures up a dubious flap of fast-food mystery meat in a flabby, ketchup-doused bap. It doesn't have to be that way. I've reclaimed the burger, and reinvented it on the way. Because very lean mince (I'm calling for pork here, but you could use lamb or beef) will produce a dry and 'bitty' burger, I've 'improved' it with a pan-fried aubergine infusion. You won't taste the aubergine; it stretches the meat (so you actually get less meat per burger – a health plus), it adds wonderful succulence to what would otherwise be a juiceless burger, and it 'carries' the flavourings – in this case, a wonderful combination of citrus, red wine and Latin-American spices. Serve in excellent-quality rolls with a salsa and a creamy dressing (see Chapter 1).

———— • ————

2–3 garlic cloves, crushed

3 tablespoons white wine vinegar

12 oz (350 g) aubergine, trimmed, peeled and diced

6 spring onions, trimmed and chopped

3 dry-pack sundried tomatoes, chopped (use scissors)

3 black olives in brine, drained and slivered off their stones

pinch or two of crushed dried chillies

juice and grated rind of ½ lime

juice and grated rind of ½ orange

1 teaspoon ground coriander

1 teaspoon ground cumin

½ pint (300 ml) stock

2 fl oz (50 ml) dry red wine

12 oz (350 g) extra-lean minced pork

2 tablespoons breadcrumbs

1½ tablespoons very low fat fromage frais

2 tablespoons tomato purée

salt and freshly ground pepper, to taste

———— • ————

1. Combine the garlic and wine vinegar in a small bowl, and set aside. Line the grill tray with foil, shiny side up. Put the grill rack in the tray. Preheat the grill to high.

2. In a frying pan, combine the aubergine, onions, sundried tomatoes, olives, chilli, lime and orange juice and rind, coriander, cumin, stock and red wine. Add the vinegar and garlic. Cover and boil for 5 minutes, then uncover, reduce the heat and simmer briskly for 3 minutes or so, until the liquid is almost gone and the aubergine is tender. Process to a rough purée in a food processor or in batches in a blender, and leave to cool.

3. Combine the minced pork with all the remaining ingredients, and stir in the aubergine infusion. Fry a tiny piece in a non-stick frying pan, taste it

for seasoning, and add salt and pepper to the mixture as needed. Form the mixture into 4–6 burgers and place them, evenly spaced, on the grill rack.

4. Grill, close to the heat, for 5–7 minutes on each side, until cooked through.

Variation

Wine-Glazed Pan-Fried Burgers

Follow steps 1, 2 and 3 of the above recipe, but don't put the burgers on a grill rack. Spray a heavy-bottomed non-stick frying pan with oil–water spray (see page 8), and heat. Brown the burgers on both sides, turning carefully with a fish slice, for 2–3 minutes. Reduce the heat a little, and fry, turning occasionally, for 3–4 minutes, then pour in 2–3 fl oz (50–75 ml) each of stock and dry red wine (it will bubble up furiously). Let the burgers cook in the liquid, turning occasionally, for 3–4 minutes, until they are beautifully glazed, the liquid is about gone, and the burgers are cooked through.

Grilled Tandoori Burgers

MAKES 4–6

SERVE these Indian-accented burgers in pita pockets, garnished with Curried Cabbage (see page 114) and a dollop of yoghurt into which you have stirred some tandoori seasoning (you'll find this on the herb and spice shelf of the supermarket).

•

3 fl oz (75 ml) very low fat yoghurt
1 tablespoon tandoori seasoning
12 oz (350 g) lean minced lamb
2 tablespoons breadcrumbs
6 oz (175 g) courgettes, trimmed and

very finely chopped (use the food
   processor)
salt and freshly ground pepper, to taste
oil–water spray (see page 8)

•

1. Preheat the grill to high.

2. Whisk the yoghurt and tandoori seasoning together and combine with the remaining ingredients, except the salt and pepper, and oil–water spray. Blend it all together very well, then fry a tiny piece in a non-stick frying pan, taste for seasoning, and add salt and pepper as needed. Form the mixture into 4–6 oval burgers.

3. Line the grill tray with foil and put the grill rack in the tray. Spray with oil–water spray, and place the burgers on the rack. Grill, 3 inches (7.5 cm) from the heat, for approximately 10 minutes on the first side and 7 minutes on the second side, until brown, crusty and cooked through, but still juicy.

Garlic–Rosemary Lamb with Mushrooms

MAKES 1½ PINTS (900 ml); SERVES 4

IT IS OFTEN possible to buy lean cubes of lamb leg in the supermarket. Trim away any little bits of surrounding fat, and use the cubes to make a quick sauté, in a pan sauce of wine, mustard, redcurrant jelly and rosemary.

▪

oil–water spray (see page 8)
1 lb (450 g) lamb leg cubes (¼ inch/
  0.5 cm), trimmed of any fat
1 garlic clove, crushed
1 tablespoon chopped fresh rosemary
  leaves
4 fl oz (100 ml) dry red wine
2 teaspoons Dijon mustard

1 teaspoon redcurrant jelly
juice of ½ lemon
¼ pint (150 ml) stock
8 oz (225 g) button mushrooms,
  quartered
dash of teriyaki sauce
salt and freshly ground pepper, to taste
chopped fresh parsley, to garnish

▪

1. Spray a heavy-bottomed frying pan with oil–water spray and heat. Dry the lamb cubes with absorbent kitchen paper, and stir-fry them in the pan for 1–2 minutes, until they have lost their raw look. Using a slotted spoon, remove the lamb to a plate.

2. Put the garlic and rosemary in the frying pan with the wine, bring to the boil, and boil for 3–5 minutes until reduced by half. Stir in the mustard, redcurrant jelly, lemon juice, stock and any juices that have accumulated under the lamb. Stir in the mushrooms, teriyaki and salt and pepper, stir, and cook for 3–4 minutes, until the mushrooms are tender, and the juices reduced to a syrupy sauce.

3. Stir in the lamb, and cook for a few minutes, until cooked through, the way you like it. Taste and adjust the seasonings, if necessary, and serve, sprinkled with chopped parsley. Serve with couscous, bulghur or rice.

Roasted Pork Tenderloin

SERVES 2–4

Pork tenderloin, when trimmed, is extremely lean and extremely delicious – if you don't overcook it! It benefits from a brief (15–20-minute) marinade, but – if you are organised enough – you could put it in to marinate in the morning, and leave it all day. The roasting time is a mere 20–25 minutes. Roasted tenderloin is a splendid component of a couscous feast: pile spiced couscous on to the centre of a platter, and surround with overlapping slices of the pork, and a vegetable stew (see page 108). Serve with Chilli Sauce (see page 15) and Olive and Cherry Tomato Relish (see page 21), and Fig and Chilli Chutney (see page 22). Under such circumstances, the pork *should* feed at least four people, but it never seems to work that way. When I have meat-eaters to dinner, they can't seem to get enough of it, so I always roast several at once. If you do the same, simply space them on the rack so that they do not touch each other. The timing should remain unchanged.

— • —

1 lb (450 g) pork tenderloin, well
  trimmed
½ quantity Honey and Mustard
  Vinaigrette (see page 25)
½ tablespoon each of ground coriander,
  cumin and paprika

ground cayenne, to taste (optional)
salt and freshly ground pepper, to taste
oil–water spray (see page 8)

— • —

1. Pierce the pork all over with a thin skewer (a cake tester is perfect). Thoroughly mix the vinaigrette with the ground spices and seasonings, and put in a non-reactive baking dish. Turn the pork in the mixture, rubbing it in well. If time permits, let marinate, turning occasionally, for 15–20 minutes. Much of the marinade will be absorbed by the pork.

2. Preheat the oven to 240°C, 475°F, Gas Mark 9. Line a shallow roasting tin with foil, shiny side up, and place a rack in the tin. Pour water into the roasting tin, to a depth of ½ inch (1 cm). Spray the rack lightly with oil–water spray, and place the pork on the rack. Roast in the oven for 20–25 minutes, turning once halfway through, and basting with the marinade. When the pork is done it will feel firm but springy, and the internal temperature will be 65–70°C (150–160°F). Let rest for 5–10 minutes, then slice thinly, crosswise, slightly on the diagonal.

Roasted Pork with Teriyaki and Sherry

SERVES 2–4

THIS IS a Chinese version of Roasted Pork Tenderloin (see page 96), to be served with rice, a huge mound of Glazed Mushrooms (see page 65), and a salad dressed with Honey and Mustard Vinaigrette (see page 25).

---

1 lb (450 g) pork tenderloin, well
  trimmed
4 fl oz (100 ml) teriyaki sauce
1 tablespoon sugar
4 fl oz (100 ml) medium dry sherry

1 garlic clove, crushed
½ inch (1 cm) piece fresh root ginger,
  peeled and crushed
oil–water spray (see page 8)

---

1. Pierce the pork all over with a thin skewer (a cake tester is perfect). Mix all the remaining ingredients, except the oil–water spray, together in a non-reactive baking dish. Turn the pork in the mixture, rubbing it in well. If time permits, let marinate, turning occasionally, for 15–20 minutes. Much of the marinade will be absorbed by the pork.

2. Preheat the oven to 240°C, 475°F, Gas Mark 9. Line a shallow roasting tin with foil, shiny side up, and place a rack in the tin. Pour water into the roasting tin, to a depth of ½ inch (1 cm). Spray the rack lightly with oil–water spray, and place the pork on the rack. Roast in the oven for 20–25 minutes, turning once halfway through, and basting with the marinade. When the pork is done, it will feel firm but springy, and the internal temperature will be 65–70°C (150–160°F). Let rest for 5–10 minutes, then slice thinly, crosswise, slightly on the diagonal.

Grilled Pork Chops (Three Ways)

PORK is bred to be lean these days. Pork loin (along with pork tenderloin) is the leanest of all pork cuts. Boneless pork loin chops must be cooked *very* quickly (until *just* done) or they will dry out. For this recipe, the chops are coated in breadcrumbs and quickly grilled so that they stay juicy. Here are three ways of preparing them – the flavourings change, but the technique remains the same. Serve with lemon or lime wedges and watercress.

•

boneless pork loin chops, ½ inch (1 cm) thick, trimmed of their rim of fat
oil–water spray (see page 8)
lemon or lime wedges and watercress, to serve

Chinese

flour, seasoned with salt, freshly ground pepper, 1 tablespoon sesame seeds and a generous pinch of ground ginger
2 egg whites, lightly beaten with ½ teaspoon each of hoisin sauce and Chinese-style chilli sauce
breadcrumbs, seasoned with salt and freshly ground pepper

Italian

flour, seasoned with salt and freshly ground pepper

2 egg whites, lightly beaten with salt, freshly ground pepper and the juice of ½ lemon
breadcrumbs, seasoned with salt, freshly ground pepper, grated rind of ½ lemon and 1 tablespoon freshly grated Parmesan cheese

French

flour, seasoned with salt and freshly ground pepper
2 egg whites, mixed to a paste with 1 tablespoon Dijon mustard
breadcrumbs, seasoned with salt, freshly ground pepper, ½ tablespoon crumbled dried tarragon and 1 tablespoon freshly grated Parmesan cheese

•

1. Dredge the chops in the appropriately seasoned flour, dip them in the seasoned egg white, then coat them in the crumbs. Place on a rack over a plate and refrigerate. (A few minutes in the fridge helps the coating to adhere.)

2. Preheat the grill to high. Spray the grill rack with oil–water spray, put the breaded chops on the rack, and spray.

3. Grill, 5 inches (12.5 cm) from the heat, for approximately 3 minutes on each side (spray the second side when you turn them), until *just* cooked through, crusty and golden. Serve the chops with lemon or lime wedges and watercress.

Chinese Dry-Fried Green Beans with Meat Sauce

MAKES ½ PINT (300 ml)

AN ABSOLUTELY gorgeous and satisfying dinner for one, served on top of a nice heap of rice (frozen microwave rice was made for times like this). In the traditional recipe, the beans are stir-fried in an ocean of oil, but you won't miss it at all. A brief squirt of sesame oil–water spray gives the requisite aroma – an ocean of the stuff would be *de trop*.

•

sesame oil–water spray (see page 8)
8 oz (225 g) stringless green beans,
   topped and tailed
4 fl oz (100 ml) stock
4 oz (110 g) lean minced pork or beef
½ teaspoon Chinese-style chilli sauce
dash of teriyaki sauce

1 tablespoon Chinese black bean sauce
1 tablespoon hoisin sauce
2 garlic cloves, crushed
1 inch (2.5 cm) piece fresh root ginger,
   peeled and crushed
5 spring onions, trimmed and sliced
2 fl oz (50 ml) medium dry sherry

•

1. Spray a non-stick wok with sesame oil–water spray and heat. Throw in the beans and stir-fry, over a high heat, for 2–3 minutes, until speckled with charred bits. Pour in 2 fl oz (50 ml) of the stock and bring to the boil. Stir-fry the beans in the boiling stock for 2–3 minutes, until they are 'crisp-tender' and the liquid is almost gone. Tip out on to a plate.

2. Stir the mince and sauces into the pan, and stir-fry for 1–1½ minutes, until the meat is cooked. Tip out on to the beans.

3. Throw the garlic, ginger, spring onions, remaining stock and sherry into the wok. Stir-fry, over high heat, for 2–3 minutes, until the liquid is almost gone and the onions are 'frying' in their own juices.

4. Return the meat, beans and any accumulated juices to the pan. Stir and cook for a few seconds to heat through and blend the flavours. Serve with rice.

Tomato Curry Beef Chow Mein

SERVES 2–4

THIS recipe is in memory of the ancient noodle houses of New York's Chinatown – haunts of my youth. Serve this fragrant tangle on a large platter, eat it out of bowls with – if at all possible – chopsticks. It makes a happy and sloppy informal meal.

•

Sauce

1 tablespoon each of soy sauce,
  Worcestershire sauce and cornflour
3 tablespoons tomato ketchup
1 teaspoon medium Madras curry
  powder
4 fl oz (100 ml) stock

Beef

8 oz (225 g) lean beef (goose (flank) skirt,
  rump skirt, fillet, or quick-fry steak),
  cut into strips
2 teaspoons cornflour
2 teaspoons soy sauce
1 tablespoon medium dry sherry
1 tablespoon water
2 garlic cloves, crushed
½ inch (1 cm) piece fresh root ginger,
  peeled and crushed
3 fl oz (75 ml) stock

Stir-fry

¼ pint (150 ml) stock
1 medium onion, cut into eighths
  (separate the layers)
1 red pepper, cored, deseeded, peeled
  (see page 9) and cut into 1 inch
  (2.5 cm) squares
8 oz (225 g) Chinese leaves, the stems
  roughly chopped and the leaves
  shredded
3 firm 'flavour' tomatoes, each cut into
  6 wedges and deseeded
⅓ package Chinese thread egg noodles,
  cooked according to package
  directions

Garnish

thinly sliced spring onions
chopped fresh coriander
sesame oil–water spray (see page 8)

•

1. Stir together all the sauce ingredients and set aside.

2. Combine the beef, cornflour, soy sauce, sherry and water, and mix well with two spoons to combine thoroughly. Set aside. Put the garlic and ginger in a small bowl.

3. Heat the 3 fl oz (75 ml) stock in a wok. Scrape in the garlic and ginger, and cook, stirring, for 1–2 minutes. Add the beef and cook, stirring, for 1½ minutes. Tip into a bowl.

4. For the stir-fry, add the ¼ pint (150 ml) stock, the onion and red pepper, and the stems of the Chinese leaves, to the wok, cover and cook, stirring,

over high heat for 2 minutes. Uncover, and stir and cook for a further 2–3 minutes until almost tender. Stir in the Chinese leaves, and cook, stirring, for a minute or so, until the leaves are wilted. Add the tomatoes, and stir and cook for 1 minute. Return the meat and its juices to the pan. Stir in the sauce and cook, stirring, for 1–2 minutes, until bubbling and thickened.

5. Add the noodles to the pan and stir until hot. To serve, garnish with spring onions, chopped coriander, and a good 'spritz' of sesame oil–water spray.

CHAPTER 7

Vegetable
Main Courses

A LOW-FAT and healthy way of life means lots and lots of lovely vegetables. What pleasure it is to keep nutrition high and fat low by feasting on an unending flow of the beautiful things. A diet rich in vegetables is colourful and full of the most wonderful contrasts of textures and tastes. This chapter contains many recipes for vegetable main dishes, and, of course, the rest of the book overflows with vegetable bounty as well. Eat vegetarian meals several days a week, and slip vegetables in everywhere you can on non-vegetarian days (see Chapter 8 for side dishes, salads, and so on) – it will improve your health, your weight, and your gastronomic pleasure.

TAKE A CAN OF BEANS . . .

Traditional bean cookery is slow – all that soaking and draining and boiling. But now, all sorts of beans come ready-cooked in cans. Baked beans are a mealtime staple, but why not take advantage of the supermarket canned bean bounty, and try some new bean dishes to serve on toast, in bowls with couscous or polenta, or as a main dish salad? It's almost as easy as opening a can of baked beans, but so much more fun!

Spicy Beans

MAKES 2 PINTS (1.1 litres)

THESE beans have verve, provided by three indispensable pantry staples: ketchup, mustard and salsa.

•

juice of 1 lime
1 pint (600 ml) stock
1 teaspoon ground cumin
1 teaspoon ground coriander
2–3 dry-pack sundried tomatoes, chopped (use scissors)
8 spring onions, trimmed and sliced
½–1 chilli, deseeded and chopped

2 garlic cloves, crushed
1½ tablespoons each of tomato salsa, tomato ketchup and mild wholegrain mustard
15 oz (425 g) can borlotti beans, drained and rinsed
15 oz (425 g) can cannellini beans, drained and rinsed

•

1. Combine half the lime juice, ½ pint (300 ml) of the stock, the spices, sundried tomatoes, onions, chilli and garlic in a large heavy-bottomed frying pan. Simmer for 4–5 minutes, until the liquid is almost gone and the onions and garlic are 'frying' in their own juices.

2. Add the remaining stock and boil for 3–4 minutes, until reduced by half. Stir in the salsa, ketchup and mustard, and simmer, stirring, for 1 minute.

3. Stir in the beans and the remaining lime juice, and simmer gently, stirring occasionally, for 3–5 minutes. Serve on toast, wrap in tortillas (with salsa garnish) or eat in bowls with couscous or polenta.

Bean Chilli

MAKES 2 PINTS (1.1 litres)

WHEN I visit my son, I often come bearing beans, usually this chilli. He was a bean-loving boy, and he has grown up to be a bean-loving man. We were dining on these beans (wrapped in tortillas, garnished with tomato salsa and pea purée – absolutely gorgeous!) when I mentioned (in passing as it were) the wind-inducing property of beans. 'I thought that was a myth,' said he. I suppose that goes to show (anecdotal evidence does count for something, after all) that the more you eat, the *less* you . . . Well, you know what I mean.

—————— • ——————

2 red onions, chopped
2–3 garlic cloves, crushed
3 dry-pack sundried tomatoes, chopped
   (use scissors)
pinch or two of crushed dried chillies
2 teaspoons ground cumin
1 teaspoon ground coriander
13 fl oz (375 ml) stock

two 15 oz (425 g) cans borlotti beans,
   drained and rinsed
¼ pint (150 ml) passata
salt and freshly ground pepper, to taste
juice of 1 lime
2 tablespoons each of chopped fresh
   parsley, mint and coriander

—————— • ——————

1. Combine the onions, garlic, tomatoes, spices and ½ pint (300 ml) of the stock in a large, heavy-bottomed frying pan. Cover and boil for 5–7 minutes, then uncover and simmer briskly for 3–4 minutes, until the onions are tender and the liquid almost gone.

2. Stir in all the remaining ingredients, except the lime juice and fresh herbs. Simmer, partially covered, for 10 minutes, or until thick and savoury. Stir in the lime juice and the herbs. Taste, and adjust the seasonings if necessary.

Black-Eyed Bean and Corn Salad

MAKES 1½ PINTS (900 ml)

BEANS and corn together offer a full complement of amino acids (the building blocks of protein), and so this is a time-honoured gastronomic marriage – a particularly happy one for vegetarians. Both beans and sweet-corn take well to the canning process – what a pleasure to be able to put something like this together in no time at all.

■

1–2 garlic cloves, crushed
½ red onion, diced
juice of ½ lime
3 fl oz (75 ml) balsamic vinegar
1 teaspoon caster sugar
15 oz (425 g) can black-eyed beans, drained and rinsed
7 oz (200 g) can extra-sweet sweetcorn kernels, drained
3 carrots, diced
3 stalks of celery, diced

1 red pepper, cored, deseeded, peeled (see page 9) and diced, or use canned or bottled peppers
3 tablespoons chopped fresh parsley
3 tablespoons chopped fresh coriander
salt and freshly ground pepper, to taste

To serve
dark greens (e.g. baby spinach leaves, rocket or watercress)
cherry tomatoes, halved

■

1. Mix the garlic, onion, lime juice, vinegar and sugar in the bottom of a large bowl and let marinate while you prepare the remaining ingredients.

2. Add all the remaining ingredients, except the greens and tomatoes, and gently stir together.

3. To serve, line a platter with greens, top with the beans and surround with halved cherry tomatoes.

Butter Bean and Bacon Stew

MAKES 1 PINT (600 ml)

THE TENDER, meaty texture of butter beans allows them to soak up pungent seasonings, and to be served as a hearty and satisfying main course. Spoon the stew into bowls and serve with crusty bread for dunking and mopping up the sauce in the bottom of the bowl. Alternatively, lavish the stew over slices of toast.

▪

olive oil–water spray (see page 8)
3 rashers lean smoked back bacon,
   trimmed of fat and diced (use scissors)
1 red onion, roughly diced
1 carrot, roughly diced
1 red pepper, cored, deseeded, peeled
   (see page 9) and roughly chopped
2 dry-pack sundried tomatoes, roughly
   diced (use scissors)
1 garlic clove, crushed

2 fl oz (50 ml) red wine
½ pint (300 ml) stock
½ teaspoon dried tarragon, crumbled
two 15 oz (425 g) cans butter beans,
   drained and rinsed
1 tablespoon mild mustard
1 tablespoon tomato purée
salt and freshly ground pepper, to taste
3 tablespoons chopped fresh parsley

▪

1. Mist a heavy-bottomed frying pan with olive oil–water spray, and heat. Sauté the bacon pieces in the pan for a minute or so, until browned. Scoop out and reserve.

2. Throw the vegetables (including the sundried tomatoes and garlic) into the pan, and pour in the red wine. Bring to the boil, and let boil for about 2 minutes, stirring and scraping up the browned deposits in the pan, until the liquid is about gone.

3. Stir in half the stock and the tarragon, cover and simmer briskly for 5 minutes. Uncover and simmer, stirring occasionally, for approximately 5 minutes, until the vegetables are very tender and the liquid about gone. Stir in the beans and the remaining stock, and bring to a simmer.

4. Whisk together the mustard and tomato purée, and stir into the beans. Season to taste, and simmer gently for 5–7 minutes, until thickened and savoury. Sprinkle with parsley and serve.

Rice-and-Lentil-Stuffed Mushrooms

MAKES 4

IF YOU don't always have cooked rice on hand, and you are in a constant rush, you might think about keeping frozen rice in the freezer. Some brands (especially the one that comes packed in individual sachets for the microwave) are not bad at all, and are ideal for a mixture like this. Canned lentils are good here, too. These enormous stuffed mushrooms make a satisfyingly meaty (although meatless) main course.

———— • ————

oil–water spray (see page 8)
4 large, flat mushrooms
2 fl oz (50 ml) red wine
dash of teriyaki or soy sauce
2 fl oz (50 ml) stock
6 tablespoons cooked rice
6 tablespoons cooked lentils

½ tablespoon chopped fresh mixed herbs
  (e.g. rosemary, thyme, oregano and
  parsley)
salt and freshly ground pepper, to taste
3 tablespoons freshly grated Parmesan
  cheese

———— • ————

1. Preheat the grill to high, and line the grill tray with foil, shiny side up. Put the grill rack in the grill tray and spray with oil–water spray.

2. Cut the stems out of the mushrooms and set aside. Put the mushrooms, gill sides up, on the grill rack and spray lightly. Grill for 2–3 minutes. If the mushrooms are very large, turn them over, spray lightly again, and grill for ½–1 minute on the second side, until cooked but not floppy.

3. Chop the mushroom stems and combine them in a frying pan with the wine, teriyaki or soy sauce, stock and any juices in the grill pan. Simmer briskly for 3–4 minutes, until the mushroom pieces are tender and the liquid almost gone. Stir in the rice, lentils and herbs, and season with salt and pepper.

4. Divide the mixture between the four grilled mushrooms, sprinkle evenly with Parmesan, and grill for 2–3 minutes, until golden.

PREVIOUS PAGE Duck Fajitas (page 88) with an accompanying bowl of Simple Tomato Salsa (page 19)

OPPOSITE Raspberry and Chocolate Puddings (page 133)

FRESH VEGETABLE STEWS

A well-seasoned rustic vegetable stew is my idea of a perfect meal. Served with a good grain (such as couscous, rice or polenta) and a garnish of Herbed Goat's Cheese Raita (see page 14), it will nourish both body and soul with great panache.

Vegetable Stew

MAKES 3½ PINTS (2.1 litres)

SERVE this Moroccan-inspired chunky stew with couscous. (Cook the couscous according to the method on page 53, but add ½ teaspoon each of ground cinnamon, cumin and coriander to the stock.) Serve Chilli Sauce (see page 15) and Fig and Chilli Chutney (see page 22) on the side.

————— • —————

2 red onions, cut into chunks
2 carrots, cut into chunks
2 garlic cloves, crushed
2 black olives in brine, drained and
  slivered off their stones
3 tablespoons sultanas
1 teaspoon ground cumin
1 teaspoon ground paprika
¼ teaspoon ground ginger
juice of 1 lemon

approximately 1 pint (600 ml) stock
4 new potatoes, quartered
salt and freshly ground pepper, to taste
2 courgettes, trimmed and chopped into
  1 inch (2.5 cm) pieces
14 oz (400 g) can chopped tomatoes
15 oz (425 g) can chick peas, drained
3 tablespoons chopped fresh parsley
3 tablespoons chopped fresh coriander

————— • —————

1. Combine the onions, carrots, garlic, olives, sultanas, spices, lemon juice and ½ pint (300 ml) of the stock in a frying pan. Simmer briskly, covered, for 10 minutes, then uncover and simmer briskly for 4–5 minutes, until the liquid is almost gone and the vegetables and spices are 'frying' in their own juices.

2. Add the potatoes and some more stock. Cook, stirring, for 3–4 minutes, until the potatoes are almost tender. Season with salt and pepper. Stir in the courgettes, a little more stock and the tomatoes. Simmer for 7–10 minutes, until all the vegetables are tender. Stir in the chick peas and herbs, and heat through. Serve with couscous.

Spicy Ratatouille

MAKES 2 PINTS (1.1 litres)

RATATOUILLE vegetables – aubergines, peppers, onions, courgettes, tomatoes – meld together to form a heavenly stew; why not give them a burnish of Mexican seasoning? I like the aubergine and peppers to be meltingly tender, but the courgettes to retain some texture, therefore the aubergine and peppers are cooked with the onions and spices, but the courgettes are added later with the canned tomatoes. Serve this ratatouille wrapped in wheat tortillas with tomato salsa, chopped raw red onion, and slivers of half-fat mozzarella.

•

1 tablespoon paprika
½ tablespoon ground cumin
½ tablespoon ground coriander
¼ teaspoon ground cinnamon
¼ teaspoon ground allspice
pinch or two of cayenne pepper
pinch of sugar
1 red onion, cut into chunks
3 black olives in brine, drained and
   slivered off their stones
3 dry-pack sundried tomatoes, diced (use
   scissors)
3 garlic cloves, crushed
1 small aubergine, peeled and cut into
   chunks

1 red pepper, cored, deseeded, peeled
   (see page 9) and cut into chunks
1 yellow pepper, cored, deseeded, peeled
   (see page 9) and cut into chunks
½ pint (300 ml) stock
4 fl oz (100 ml) dry red wine
2 medium courgettes (1 green, 1 yellow,
   if possible), trimmed and cut into
   chunks
14 oz (400 g) can tomatoes, drained and
   cut into strips
salt and freshly ground pepper, to taste
1–2 tablespoons chopped fresh mixed
   herbs (e.g. parsley, basil and oregano)

•

1. Combine the spices, sugar, onion, olives, sundried tomatoes, garlic, aubergine and peppers in a heavy-bottomed frying pan or wok. Add half the stock and the wine, cover, bring to the boil, and boil for 5–7 minutes. Uncover and simmer, stirring, for about a further 5 minutes, until the aubergine is tender and the contents of the pan are 'frying' in their own juices.

2. Add the courgettes and remaining stock, and stir to mix. Simmer for a few minutes. Add the canned tomatoes and simmer, partially covered, for approximately 10 minutes more, until all the vegetables are tender. Taste, adjust the seasonings if necessary, and stir in the herbs.

Potato Vegetable Stew

MAKES 2½ PINTS (1.4 litres)

LARGE, flat, open mushrooms deliver an almost wild flavour, and the onion–garlic–olive infusion gives a Mediterranean dimension. The potatoes soak it all up nicely. Serve in bowls garnished with Herbed Goat's Cheese Raita (see page 14).

---

2 red onions, chopped

2 garlic cloves, crushed

pinch or two of crushed dried chillies

3–4 black olives in brine, drained and slivered off their stones

2–3 dry-pack sundried tomatoes, chopped (use scissors)

4 fl oz (100 ml) dry red wine

4 fl oz (100 ml) stock

1 lb (450 g) all-purpose potatoes, peeled and cut into ½ inch (1 cm) chunks

8 oz (225 g) large, flat mushrooms, coarsely chopped

salt and freshly ground pepper, to taste

1¼ lb (550 g) courgettes, trimmed and cut into ½ inch (1 cm) chunks

10 oz (275 g) fresh tomatoes (about 3 medium), peeled, deseeded and cut into strips

2–3 tablespoons chopped fresh parsley

---

1. Combine the onions, garlic, chilli, olives, sundried tomatoes, red wine and stock in a heavy-bottomed frying pan or non-stick wok. Cover, and simmer for 5–7 minutes, then uncover, and simmer for a further 3–4 minutes, until the onions are tender.

2. Stir in the potatoes and mushrooms, and season with salt and pepper. Simmer, stirring, for approximately 5 minutes, until the potatoes are half cooked. Stir in the courgettes, and cook for 2–3 minutes.

3. Stir in the fresh tomatoes, and simmer for 7–10 minutes, until all the vegetables are tender, and the tomatoes have cooked down to a sauce. Taste, adjust the seasonings if necessary, and stir in the parsley.

· CHAPTER 8 ·

Vegetable Accompaniments and Light Meals

VEGETABLES not only add nutrition to a meal, but colour, textural interest and general pizzazz as well. They dress up simply grilled fish, chicken and meat beautifully, but put them together occasionally, without the hunks of animal protein, for a dazzling vegetarian feast. Walk through an outdoor food market, or amble down the greengrocery aisle of your local supermarket for inspiration – the vegetables glow with potential and practically beg to be taken home.

Creamy Mushroom Ragout

MAKES 1½ PINTS (900 ml)

NO-FAT mushroom sautés are richly delicious made with stock, teriyaki (or soy) sauce and dry sherry. In this sauté, the mushrooms are creamy, the result of adding Dijon mustard. Simmering eliminates the sinus-blasting properties of the mustard, and leaves a gently spicy creaminess. Serve on toast, as a vegetable accompaniment, or as part of a vegetable dinner.

---

4 fl oz (100 ml) stock
2 fl oz (50 ml) medium dry sherry
several dashes of teriyaki sauce
2 lb (900 g) mixed mushrooms (e.g. brown cap, shiitakes trimmed of their stems, button mushrooms, etc.), cleaned and cut into quarters

6 spring onions, trimmed and sliced
½ teaspoon dried tarragon, crumbled
2 rounded tablespoons Dijon mustard (or Provençale mustard with garlic and red peppers, if possible)
freshly ground pepper, to taste

---

1. Combine the stock, sherry, teriyaki, mushrooms, onions and tarragon in a frying pan. Simmer, stirring occasionally, for 5–7 minutes, until the mushrooms have exuded a great deal of liquid.

2. Stir in the mustard, season with pepper, and continue simmering for 3–4 minutes, until the mushrooms are tender, and bathed in a creamy sauce.

Pan-Braised Fennel

SERVES 4

RAW FENNEL is crisp, refreshing and makes an absolutely gorgeous, anise-flavoured component of a salad or crudité assortment. As a cooked vegetable, it is superb. Serve as a vegetable accompaniment, or give polenta a subtle scent of anise, by chopping up this pan-braised fennel and stirring it into the polenta in step 2 of the method on page 55.

2–3 bulbs fennel
salt and freshly ground pepper, to taste

approximately 4 fl oz (100 ml) stock
juice of 1 lemon

---

1. Trim the tough outer layers off the fennel bulbs, and remove the stalks and leaves. Save the fronds for garnish. Trim a little off the bottom of each bulb, but leave the cores intact. Cut each bulb in half lengthwise, then cut the halves into wedges or quarters.

2. Spread the fennel in a heavy-bottomed frying pan, season with salt and pepper, then pour in 2–3 fl oz (50–75 ml) stock and half the lemon juice. Cover, and simmer briskly for 10 minutes, uncovering to stir them up occasionally. Let the liquid cook away, so that the fennel begins to brown and catch. Pour in a little more stock and lemon juice, and keep cooking for 3–5 minutes, until the fennel is browned, glazed and tender. Sprinkle with snipped fennel fronds, and serve.

Pan-Braised Carrots

MAKES 1 PINT (600 ml)

PAN BRAISING is a marvellous, moderately quick way of getting lots of flavour into vegetables, and making the most of their own good flavour.

——— ∎ ———

1 lb (450 g) carrots, quartered
juice of ½ orange
juice of ½ lemon
½ tablespoon balsamic vinegar
several dashes of teriyaki sauce
several dashes of Tabasco sauce

7–10 whole garlic cloves, unpeeled
approximately 1 pint (600 ml) stock
salt and freshly ground pepper, to taste
additional lemon and orange juice
1–2 tablespoons chopped fresh herbs
  (mint or parsley)

——— ∎ ———

1. Combine the carrots, citrus juices, balsamic vinegar, teriyaki and Tabasco sauces, garlic and approximately 5 fl oz (150 ml) stock in a heavy-bottomed or non-stick frying pan. Season with salt and pepper, cover, and simmer for 7–10 minutes, shaking the pan and stirring it all up occasionally.

2. Uncover the pan, add another 2–3 fl oz (50–75 ml) stock, and simmer briskly for 8–10 minutes until the carrots are *very* tender and glazed, the garlic soft, and the liquid about gone. Add more stock during cooking, as needed. Squeeze in a bit more lemon and orange juice at the very end of cooking, and sprinkle with chopped herbs.

Curried Cabbage

MAKES 1 PINT (600 ml)

THIS is a quick and easy spicy cabbage stir-fry to serve as a vegetable side dish, or as a garnish for the Grilled Tandoori Burgers on page 94. Or try a wonderful vegetarian sandwich: stuff the cabbage into a pita pocket with a dollop of Herbed Goat's Cheese Raita (see page 14) and a dab of chutney. (Call me strange, but I *do* love a good cabbage sandwich!)

■

1 large onion, halved and cut into thin half moons
2 garlic cloves, crushed
¼ teaspoon each of mild chilli powder, ground cinnamon, ground turmeric and ground ginger
pinch of ground allspice

1 teaspoon paprika
1 teaspoon ground cumin
½ teaspoon ground coriander
1 pint (600 ml) stock
12 oz (350 g) shredded white cabbage
juice of 1 lime or lemon
salt and freshly ground pepper, to taste

■

1. Combine the onion, garlic, spices and ½ pint (300 ml) stock in a heavy-bottomed frying pan. Cover, and boil for 5–7 minutes, then reduce the heat a little and simmer, stirring frequently, for 3–5 minutes, until the vegetables and spices are 'frying' in their own juices.

2. Stir in the cabbage and remaining stock, and simmer, uncovered, for 15–20 minutes, until the cabbage is tender and the sauce is thick and savoury. Squeeze in the lime or lemon juice until the taste of the cabbage is vivid and bracing. Taste, and season with salt and pepper if necessary.

Note

1 tablespoon tandoori seasoning, or mild Korma curry powder, could be used in place of all the spices.

Stir-Fried Courgettes

STIR-FRY vegetables in stock and lemon or lime juice instead of oil or butter. The citrus juice helps to glaze the vegetables as well as imparting a pleasant tang; sundried tomatoes, garlic, chillies and olives ensure that the stir-fry will not be bland. This is a method rather than a calibrated recipe; adapt it to other vegetables, such as carrots, peeled peppers, Jerusalem arti-chokes, cauliflower florets, and peeled, sliced broccoli stalks.

———— ∎ ————

courgettes, trimmed and cut into 1 inch
    (2.5 cm) dice
crushed garlic
dry-pack sundried tomatoes, snipped (use
    scissors)
2–3 black olives in brine, drained and
    slivered off their stones

pinch or two of crushed dried chillies
stock
lemon or lime juice
salt and freshly ground pepper
chopped fresh parsley and shredded basil
    leaves, to serve

———— ∎ ————

1. Put the courgettes in a wok with all the remaining ingredients, except the fresh herbs. For a panful of courgettes, you will need approximately 4 fl oz (100 ml) stock and the juice of ½ lemon or lime.

2. Cook, stirring, over high heat, for 5–7 minutes, until the courgettes are tender, and the liquid about gone. If necessary, add a little more liquid as the courgettes cook. Sprinkle with herbs, and serve.

Pan-Roasted Potatoes

MAKES 1½ PINTS (900 ml)

THIS new method of roasting potatoes in a frying pan on the hob, with highly flavoured seasonings, has become one of my pet techniques – I make one or another version of it several times a week. The potatoes go well with fish, chicken or meat (as potatoes always do) but they also serve as a splendid focus of a vegetarian meal – try them with Creamy Mushroom Ragout and Pan-braised Fennel (see page 112).

---

1 lb (450 g) small, waxy, oval potatoes, such as Charlotte
juice of 1 lemon
approximately 10 fl oz (300 ml) stock
3 oz (75 g) dry-pack sundried tomatoes, cut into strips (use scissors)

approximately 10 large garlic cloves, unpeeled
3 black olives in brine, drained and slivered off their stones
several dashes of Tabasco sauce
several dashes of Worcestershire sauce

---

1. Halve the potatoes lengthwise, and spread in a heavy-bottomed non-stick frying pan, cut side up. Squeeze in the lemon juice, and add approximately 5 fl oz (150 ml) stock. Scatter in the sundried tomatoes, garlic, and olive pieces, and dash in the sauces. Cover, and simmer briskly for 5–7 minutes, shaking the pan and stirring the potatoes occasionally, until they are approximately half done.

2. Uncover the pan and continue to simmer briskly for about 10 minutes. As the liquid cooks away, the potatoes will catch and brown a bit. Replenish the pan, with a little more stock as this happens, loosening the browned bits with your wooden spoon as you do so. When the potatoes are cooked through, they should be glazed, sticky, and wonderfully tender, but not crumbled or broken up. Serve hot or warm.

Golden Spice Pan-Roasted Potatoes

MAKES 1½ PINTS (900 ml)

———— ▪ ————

1 lb (450 g) small, waxy, oval potatoes,
   such as Charlotte
juice of 1 lemon
approximately 10 fl oz (300 ml) stock
approximately 10 large garlic cloves,
   unpeeled

1 teaspoon ground tumeric
2 teaspoons ground cumin
2 teaspoons ground coriander
several dashes of Tabasco sauce
several dashes of Worcestershire sauce
salt and freshly ground pepper to taste

———— ▪ ————

1. Prepare and cook the potatoes as in the Pan-Roasted Potatoes recipe on page 116, mixing in the spices in step 1.

2. At the end of cooking, taste, and squeeze in a little more lemon juice, to your taste.

Flavour of Mexico Pan-Roasted Potatoes

MAKES 1½ PINTS (900 ml)

———— ▪ ————

1 lb (450 g) small, waxy, oval potatoes,
   such as Charlotte
juice of 1–2 limes
2 teaspoons ground cumin
2 teaspoons ground coriander
1 large red chilli, deseeded and cut into
   strips

1 large green chilli, deseeded and cut
   into strips
salt and freshly ground pepper, to taste
approximately 2 tablespoons chopped
   fresh coriander

———— ▪ ————

1. Prepare and cook the potatoes as in the Pan-Roasted Potatoes recipe on page 116, substituting lime juice for the lemon juice, and adding the spices and chilli strips in step 1.

2. To serve, squeeze on a little more lime juice, season with salt and pepper, and scatter on the coriander.

Goat's Cheese Salad with Warm Pan-Roasted Potatoes

I COULD eat (I have eaten!) large quantities of this. Any of the pan-roasted potato recipes (see pages 116–117) would do nicely here. Serve it as a first course, or make a meal of it.

———— ∎ ————

croûtons (thin slices of baguette)
medium-fat goat's cheese (in little pots)
greens (e.g. herb salad, lamb's lettuce,
   rocket leaves, watercress, etc.)

Red Pepper Mustard Vinaigrette (see
   page 24)
Pan-Roasted Potatoes (see
   pages 116–117)

———— ∎ ————

1. For each serving, spread 2–3 croûtons with goat's cheese. Grill for 2–3 minutes until speckled with brown.

2. Toss a good handful of greens with some of the vinaigrette. Spread on a plate and top with the croûtons. Surround with some of the potatoes. Sprinkle with parsley and serve at once.

Deconstructed Potato Salad

For a convivial, informal and entertaining potato feast or first course, steam a quantity of small new potatoes, and pile them – warm or at room temperature – into a rustic pottery bowl. Set bowls of well-chosen dips, swirls, spreads and dressings (see suggestions below) on the table as well. Set out bowls of cherry tomatoes, sliced or diced red onion, and chopped herbs. Let everyone take varying combinations of ingredients and dip, swirl and spread to their hearts' content.

Dips, Swirls, Dressings, etc.
Herbed Goat's Cheese Raita (see page 14); Vinaigrettes (see pages 23–26); Chilli Swirl or Sauce (see page 15); White Bean Swirl or Dip (see page 16); Beetroot Purée (see page 13)

Mediterranean Salad

A DAZZLING salad in every way, this adds incandescence to any dinner party or buffet. Alternatively, serve it on an ordinary day for a quick dose of gastronomic colour therapy.

———— • ————

rocket leaves or baby spinach leaves
char-grilled peppers, cored, deseeded,
   peeled (see page 9) and cut into
   2 inch (5 cm) wide strips
'flavour' tomatoes, cut into quarters or
   eighths, depending on size

chopped fresh parsley
shredded fresh basil
Red Pepper Mustard Vinaigrette (see
   page 24)

———— • ————

1. Line a platter with rocket or baby spinach leaves. Drape the pepper strips here and there, and pile the tomatoes in the centre. Sprinkle with parsley and basil.

2. Drizzle some vinaigrette over the salad, and serve the rest separately.

Oriental Beetroot Salad

MAKES ½ PINT (300 ml)

MORE colour therapy; this time of a darker, earthier hue. Circle this salad around the tuna on page 74, or tip it into a spicy, slippery pile on a mass of dark greens.

---■---

9 oz (250 g) vacuum-packed cooked
  beetroot (no vinegar)
2 spring onions, trimmed and sliced
1 garlic clove, crushed
1 inch (2.5 cm) piece fresh root ginger,
  peeled and crushed
juice and grated rind of ½ orange

juice and grated rind of ½ lime
½ teaspoon teriyaki sauce
1 teaspoon chilli sauce
1 teaspoon balsamic vinegar
1 tablespoon chopped fresh coriander
1 tablespoon chopped fresh parsley

---■---

1. Open the package of beetroot, and drain the juices into a small frying pan. Slice the beetroot and put the slices into a bowl.

2. Add all the remaining ingredients, except the fresh herbs, to the frying pan, and boil for 2–3 minutes, until reduced by half.

3. Pour this scant sauce over the beetroot and stir so that the slices are coated. To serve, spread on a serving plate and sprinkle with fresh herbs.

CHAPTER 9

Desserts

TRADITIONAL high-fat dessert ingredients – butter, cream, crème fraîche, mascarpone cheese, egg yolks, suet – are so rich, fatty and cloying, that my gut spasms and my heart burns just thinking about them. Fortunately, low-fat desserts are sheer pleasure. Fruit, fruit juices, flavour extracts, low-fat dairy products (quark, fromage frais, ricotta cheese), high-cocoa-solid chocolate and low-fat cocoa powder, liqueurs – with such a rich and varied palette of ingredients, low-fat desserts vibrate with clear, fresh flavours. They are light and refreshing without being insubstantial; creamy and unctuous without ever being over-rich, stodgy or cloying.

The recipes begin on page 125, but don't skip The Dessert Storecupboard section on pages 122–4 as it contains ideas for almost instant low-fat desserts.

THE DESSERT STORECUPBOARD

Natural vanilla extract   the real thing, evocatively sweet and perfumed, available through mail order (see page 138). The more readily available vanilla *essence* is, alas, acrid and harsh. It really is worth stocking up on the real thing.

Jams, marmalades, preserves and conserves   I find that these, used as sweeteners in various low-fat desserts, add a much more complex depth of flavour than plain sugar. Keep an interesting variety in the store-cupboard – orange and lemon marmalade; wild blueberry, cherry or blackberry conserves; raspberry jam, etc. – and all sorts of quick, impromptu puddings are just moments away. Honey and maple syrup also provide complex flavour along with their sweetness.

Amaretti biscuits   these Italian almond-flavoured biscuits (although they have a strong almond taste) actually contain no high-fat almonds, making them incredibly useful to a low-fat cook. Crush them into fragrant crumbs to provide an almond-scented crunch factor to various puddings.

Sponge fingers and trifle sponges   perfect for tiramisu and trifle-type puddings, these contain some whole eggs but no other added fat, so – although not *no*-fat – they are relatively *low* fat.

Liqueurs, spirits and wine   particularly Cointreau (orange-flavoured), Crème de Pêche (peach-flavoured), Amaretto (almond-flavoured), red vermouth and rum to add subtle fragrance to your desserts.

Chocolate   without chocolate the world would be a much sadder place. I always say that chocolate is an essential nutrient. It isn't really, of course, but – for some of us – it certainly seems so, at least on a visceral/spiritual level. What on earth am I talking about? Other chocolate-lovers will know about that deep chocolate passion we all experience. Fortunately, lower-fat chocolate desserts are absolutely splendid. Stock up on low-fat cocoa powder (deep, intense, chocolaty) and high-cocoa-solid (70 per cent) whole chocolate. These heady, deep dark products will reach places you didn't even know you had! (See page 138 for mail-order availability.)

Frozen fruit   at the time of writing, frozen raspberries and frozen blueberries (how many other *blue* foods can you think of?) are widely available (and hopefully more varieties will be soon). Bring them home in a cool bag and stock up your freezer. And freeze fruit yourself, on non-stick trays (then gather up into plastic bags) – mango cubes; sliced, peeled, ripe bananas; cubed peaches and pears; halved strawberries, etc. Use the berries to make coulis (see page 128), and use any of the frozen fruit to make **quick ice cream**: put ¾–1 lb (350–450 g) hard frozen berries or fruit pieces in a food processor, add 1 tablespoon low-fat fromage frais and 1 tablespoon fruit preserve, conserve or marmalade (less for mango cubes and banana slices), and process until perfectly smooth. As it processes, add more conserve or preserve to taste, if needed, along with a dash of vanilla extract. Eat at once.

Fruit fruit in general makes the fastest pudding imaginable. When fruit is ripe, seasonal, perfumed, bursting with juice, you don't need to do much to it to make it perfect – just eat it! A perfectly ripe melon, for instance, halved (scoop out the seeds) and filled to overflowing with fresh raspberries or diced ripe peaches can hardly be bettered. Or make a luxurious fruit salad by dressing berries and ripe fruit with a mixture of orange juice, a dash or two of Cointreau and Crème de Pêche, and a teaspoon of vanilla extract. Or serve ripe but firm half mangoes, scored and turned inside out (see page 10) with wedges of lime alongside.

Dried fruits an assortment, including cranberries, cherries, blueberries, apricots, figs, prunes, etc., quickly simmered with fruit juices and liqueurs, make wonderful compotes.

Dairy products ricotta cheese (15 per cent fat); quark (0 per cent fat); fromage frais (0 per cent fat). Keep these in the fridge (the quark can also be frozen) and – along with your store-cupboard ingredients and a choice of fresh or frozen fruit – you will have an infinite number of almost instant dessert possibilities at all times. These three invaluable dairy products, alone or in combination, can be processed into excellent creamy toppings to use instead of whipped cream, crème fraîche or sour cream. Try some of the following:

1. Whisk together 8 oz (225 g) no-fat fromage frais with approximately (to taste) 1 tablespoon honey or maple syrup and 1 teaspoon vanilla extract.

2. Blend together (in a food processor) 8 oz (225 g) ricotta (or half ricotta, half no-fat fromage frais), approximately (to taste) 1 tablespoon marmalade or conserve. For example, blend in wild blueberry conserve to achieve a misty lilac cloud of cream – perfect for dolloping on top of fresh berries, especially blueberries.

3. In a food processor, blend a perfectly ripe peeled mango, or two perfectly ripe peeled peaches, into 8 oz (225 g) ricotta for an intense and creamy fruit mousse.

4. Make a chocolate cream by processing (in a food processor again) 6 oz (175 g) each of ricotta and quark with 3 tablespoons icing sugar, 1 tablespoon low-fat cocoa powder, ½ oz (15 g) melted and slightly cooled high-cocoa-solid dark chocolate, and ½ teaspoon vanilla extract. Serve as a topping for poached pears or stoned fresh cherries, or serve in goblets, each topped with an amaretti biscuit.

Frozen yoghurt   the low-fat foodie's answer to rich designer ice creams are starting to appear in freezer cabinets all over the place. Look for tubs of low-fat frozen yoghurt tucked in between the butter-fat-laden premium ice creams. The yoghurts range from 0 per cent to 3 per cent fat, but the texture is rich and creamy enough to satisfy the most rabid ice cream fan. Keep several tubs in the freezer for wonderful quick puds. I usually zap it in the microwave for a few seconds to soften it slightly (except when the topping is to be hot) and then dress it up a bit. Here are a few examples:

1. Top with Raspberry Coulis (see page 128). Scatter on some fresh raspberries as well if they are in season. Vanilla or raspberry frozen yoghurts work best here.

2. Melt some high-cocoa-solid chocolate (see page 122), then drizzle the hot chocolate over a couple of scoops of frozen yoghurt. The chocolate will harden into a brittle shell when it hits the cold confection, and some of the yoghurt will begin to melt into a creamy, chocolate-dabbled puddle – sheer bliss!

3. Top with hot Banana, Rum and Raisin Sauce (see page 125).

4. Top with Hot Dried Fruit Compote (see page 130).

5. Fold crushed amaretti biscuits into slightly softened frozen yoghurt. Top with fresh berries mixed with a tablespoon or so of orange juice, a dash of vanilla extract, and a soupçon of Cointreau.

Banana, Rum and Raisin Sauce

SERVES 1

THIS is a rather dramatic way to make and serve a hot banana-raisin compote. It could also be served with homemade processor banana ice cream (see page 123), or with a ricotta cream topping (see page 123).

▪

1 ripe banana
1 tablespoon dark rum
1 tablespoon each of lemon juice, lime
  juice and orange juice

pinch of brown sugar
½ tablespoon raisins
frozen yoghurt, to serve

▪

1. Preheat the oven to 220°C, 425°F, Gas Mark 7.

2. Peel the banana and cut in half lengthwise, then cut crosswise into ½ inch (1 cm) chunks. Put the banana on the bottom half of a piece of folded and creased, then opened, heavy-duty foil.

3. Sprinkle all the remaining ingredients, except the yoghurt, evenly over the banana. Fold and crimp the foil packet all around so that no steam can escape (it should be a roomy, well-sealed pouch).

4. Put the pouch on a baking sheet and bake in the oven for 12–15 minutes.

5. To serve, put a portion of solidly frozen yoghurt in a bowl. Cut open the end of the foil packet with scissors, and then tip out the hot banana and juices over the yoghurt.

Orange-Scented Tiramisu

SERVES 6–8

TIRAMISU is the sort of pudding that low-fat devotees run from, screaming. Egg yolks, mascarpone cheese, whipped cream – help! Tiramisu means 'pick me up', but the dessert should really be called 'strike me down'. This version, however, banishes the butter, fat and egg yolks, and it also omits the booze – a sort of PG version of the Italian classic. Orange juice and orange marmalade give it a refreshing citrus fragrance.

———— • ————

15–16 sponge fingers
5 fl oz (150 ml) freshly squeezed orange
  juice
2 tablespoons Cointreau
1½ teaspoons natural vanilla extract

three 9 oz (250 g) cartons ricotta, or use
  half ricotta, half quark
2 tablespoons orange marmalade
2 oz (50 g) high-cocoa-solid dark
  chocolate, grated (see page 122)

———— • ————

1. Line the bottom of a shallow, rectangular (12 × 7 inch/30 × 18 cm) or oval baking dish with one layer of sponge fingers. (You may have to break a few in half.) Stir together the orange juice, Cointreau and ½ teaspoon of the vanilla extract. Sprinkle this mixture over the sponge fingers, a tablespoon at a time.

2. Combine the ricotta cheese, marmalade and remaining vanilla in the food processor. Taste as you go, and add more marmalade if you feel it is needed. Process until the mixture is smooth and fluffy, then spread over the sponge fingers.

3. Sprinkle the top evenly with grated chocolate, and chill until needed.

Individual Banana Tiramisus

SERVES 2

IS THIS a tiramisu, or a species of trifle? Either way, it is an unconventional but magnificent creamy banana extravaganza.

---•---

a few sponge fingers
1 large, juicy orange, halved
¾ teaspoon natural vanilla extract
several dashes of one or two liqueurs
   (e.g. Crème de Pêche and Cointreau)
1 firm, ripe banana, peeled

9 oz (250 g) carton ricotta, or use quark,
   no-fat fromage frais, or a mixture
approximately ½ tablespoon blackberry,
   cherry or blueberry conserve, or orange
   marmalade
1 pair amaretti biscuits

---•---

1. Break up the sponge fingers and distribute the pieces between two large goblets or individual glass bowls. Squeeze the juice of half the orange over the pieces, and drizzle over ½ teaspoon vanilla and the liqueurs. Stir until the biscuit pieces are rather mushy.

2. Slice the banana over the broken biscuits, and squeeze the juice from the remaining orange half over them.

3. In a processor, whip together the ricotta, conserve or marmalade and the remaining vanilla. Taste, and add a little more conserve or marmalade, if needed. Spread over the bananas.

4. Put the amaretti, in their paper cases, on your work surface. Reduce to crumbs by hitting them with a rolling pin, or the bottom of a bottle or bowl. Shake the crumbs out of the wrapper on to the surface of the puddings. Serve at once.

Instant Berry Trifles

SERVES 1

THIS is so simple to slap together (if you have the coulis on hand) but it makes a very impressive pud. The quantities given below serve one; make as many as you need. Serve as soon as they are made.

———— • ————

1 sponge finger
a few tablespoons Raspberry Coulis (see below)
several tablespoons raspberries and blueberries (fresh or thawed frozen)

9 oz (250 g) carton ricotta
approximately 1 tablespoon blueberry or cherry conserve
1 teaspoon natural vanilla extract
½ pair amaretti biscuits, crushed

———— • ————

1. Tear the sponge finger into pieces and drop it into the bottom of a large goblet or an individual glass dessert bowl. Pour on some of the coulis, and stir gently to saturate the sponge.

2. Spoon the berries over the sponge, and drizzle on a little more coulis.

3. Put the ricotta, conserve and vanilla extract in a food processor, and process to combine. Taste, and add a little more conserve, if needed. Dollop on to the berries, and sprinkle with amaretti crumbs.

Raspberry Coulis

MAKES 16 fl oz (475 ml)

THIS suave scarlet sauce goes with so many things (try it with whole strawberries for dipping) – it pays to keep it on hand at all times.

———— • ————

two 12 oz (350 g) cartons frozen raspberries, thawed

icing sugar, to taste
a few drops of lemon juice, if needed

———— • ————

1. Drain the berries and purée in a food processor or blender. Pass the purée through a nylon sieve to eliminate the pips.

2. Sweeten the coulis with icing sugar, and add a few drops of lemon juice, if necessary, to sharpen the taste. Refrigerate until needed.

Figs with Raspberries

SOMETIMES the simplest puddings are the best. If you have a fig tree, and a few raspberry canes in your garden, this is the ultimate seasonal pud.

———— ▪ ————

burstingly ripe fresh figs
fresh raspberries

Raspberry Coulis (see page 128)
fresh mint leaves

———— ▪ ————

1. Slice each fig into sixths, from top to bottom, without cutting right through the bottom, so that the figs can be opened like a flower. Fill the centre of each fig 'flower' with a generous tumble of raspberries.

2. Pour some raspberry coulis around each fig, and then decorate with mint leaves.

Sparkling Strawberries

SERVES 2

AMÉ IS a splendid non-alcoholic sparkling fruit drink; an excellent stand-in for wine and champagne for those who don't touch alcohol. I always serve it at dinner parties, and everyone seems to like it – even those who *do* drink alcohol. Mixed with strawberries (try it with raspberries as well) it makes an extremely festive and attractive simple dessert.

———— ▪ ————

9 oz (250 g) punnet strawberries
1½ tablespoons sugar
1 tablespoon snipped fresh mint

approximately 4 tablespoons white Amé
or flavoured sparkling mineral water

———— ▪ ————

1. Hull the strawberries and slice them. Mix gently with the sugar and mint, and let sit for 5 minutes.

2. Divide the strawberries between two goblets. Pour half the Amé into each, and serve at once.

Lychee and Pineapple Cooler

PEELED, cored, ripe pineapple, readily available in most supermarkets, makes a dessert like this ridiculously simple. Like the Sparkling Strawberries on page 129, it is light, fruity and refreshing – just right after a substantial and spicy meal.

———— ▪ ————

canned lychees in natural juice, chilled
prepared fresh pineapple, cubed

fresh mint springs, to decorate

———— ▪ ————

1. Put a handful of lychees and several cubes of pineapple in each glass goblet (champagne flutes are perfect).

2. Fill each glass with a few tablespoons of juice from the lychee can and a few tablespoons of the pineapple juice. Add a sprig of mint.

Cold Oranges with Hot Dried Fruit Compote

THIS is a method, rather than a recipe – the amount of each ingredient required depends on how many you plan to feed. Keep fresh, juicy seedless oranges in the freezer as a matter of course, because you'll need semi-frozen oranges here. When the urge to prepare this hot and cold extravaganza strikes, put the fruit on to simmer and then take the oranges out of the freezer. In approximately 10 minutes, although the oranges will still be partially frozen, you will be able to slice them with a sharp, serrated knife (make sure your knife is sharp, grip the orange with an oven glove, and work carefully). If, on the other hand, you have no frozen oranges in the freezer, and want to serve this as dessert after supper, put the whole oranges in the freezer when you start dinner preparations. When you are ready for them, the oranges will be partly frozen. When sliced, quickly trim the peel and pith from each slice (I use scissors) and overlap them on small plates. Spoon the hot, syrupy fragrant compote into the centre of the icy orange slices and serve *at once*. Cranberry juice is available in cartons from most supermarkets.

———— • ————

cranberry juice (approximately 8 fl oz/225
  ml per 8 oz/225 g fruit)
grated orange rind, to taste
juice and grated rind of ½ lemon (or to
  taste)
Cointreau, to taste

several handfuls of mixed dried
  cranberries, cherries (sour and bing)
  and blueberries
ice cold (partially frozen) large, juicy
  seedless oranges

———— • ————

1. Combine all the ingredients, except the oranges, in a frying pan and simmer for approximately 10 minutes, until the fruits are plump and coated in a thick syrup.

2. Quickly slice the oranges and, with kitchen scissors, trim the peel and pith from each slice. Arrange overlapping orange slices on individual chilled serving plates. Spoon some compote with its syrup over the slices, and serve *at once*.

Glazed Figs

MAKES 1 PINT (600 ml)

DRIED figs become plump, juicy and aromatic when they are simmered with spiced red vermouth. Serve with a dollop of ricotta–fromage frais cream (see page 123) that has been sweetened with orange or lemon marmalade.

———— • ————

1 lb (450 g) ready-to-eat (pre-soaked)
  dried figs
8 fl oz (225 ml) red vermouth
1 tablespoon orange-flavoured liqueur
  (Grand Marnier or Cointreau)

juice and shredded rind of ½ orange
shredded rind of ½ lemon
1 cinnamon stick
1 vanilla pod
4 fl oz (100 ml) water

———— • ————

1. Combine all the ingredients in a non-reactive saucepan.

2. Simmer briskly, stirring occasionally, for 8–10 minutes, until the liquid has reduced to a thick syrupy glaze and the figs are plump and tender. Remove the cinnamon and vanilla before serving.

Coffee-Cup Chocolate Soufflés

MAKES 8

ADORABLE little mini-soufflés, rising dramatically out of their coffee cups – life *is* good! Put them in the oven at dinner time and they will be ready at pudding time. They can also be made in advance, left to subside a bit, and turned on to a bed of raspberry sauce (see variation below). For all their heady, deep, dark chocolate intensity, these are very low-fat indeed and low-sugar as well; each soufflé contains only a little more than 1 table-spoon of sugar.

---

9 tablespoons caster sugar
9 tablespoons unsweetened, fat-reduced
  cocoa powder
9 egg whites, at room temperature
pinch of cream of tartar

½ oz (15 g) high-cocoa-solid dark
  chocolate, grated
1½ teaspoons natural vanilla extract
1½ teaspoons dark rum

---

1. Preheat the oven to 180°C, 350°F, Gas Mark 4. Remove the top oven shelf. Put the kettle on to boil.

2. Set aside 2 tablespoons sugar and sift the remainder together with all of the cocoa. Set aside.

3. Using an electric mixer, beat the egg whites with the cream of tartar until foamy. At highest speed, continue beating, adding the remaining 2 tablespoons plain sugar, a little at a time, until the whites hold stiff peaks.

4. With a rubber spatula, fold the sugar–cocoa mixture into the beaten whites. Fold in the chocolate, vanilla and rum.

5. Divide the mixture between eight 6 fl oz (175 ml) ovenproof tea or coffee cups. Put them in a baking dish (already placed in the centre of the oven) that will hold them in one uncrowded layer, and pour boiling water into the dish to come halfway up the sides of the cups.

6. Bake the soufflés for approximately 30 minutes. They are done when they are extravagantly puffed, and a cake tester inserted gently into one of the cracks emerges not quite clean. (They should remain somewhat gooey and fudgey.) Serve at once.

Variation

Little Chocolate Puddings

Let the cups cool on a wire rack. The little soufflés will collapse (but not as much as you think they will). When cooled and collapsed, loosen all around with a knife and turn each one out on to a puddle of Raspberry Coulis (see page 128) on a plate. Scatter around some fresh raspberries and add, if you wish, a dollop of ricotta cream (see page 123).

Raspberry and Chocolate Puddings

MAKES 4

———— ▪ ————

Raspberry Compote

12 oz (350 g) carton frozen raspberries, thawed
1 tablespoon cornflour
6–7 tablespoons sugar (to taste)
grated rind of ½ lemon
grated rind and juice of ½ orange
½ teaspoon natural vanilla extract

Soufflé Topping

4 tablespoons caster sugar
4 tablespoons unsweetened, fat-reduced cocoa powder
4 egg whites, at room temperature
pinch of cream of tartar
½ oz (15 g) high-cocoa-solid dark chocolate, grated
1 teaspoon natural vanilla extract
1 teaspoon Cointreau

———— ▪ ————

1. Preheat the oven to 200°C, 400°F, Gas Mark 6.

2. Drain the juice from the berries into a bowl, add the cornflour, and stir to dissolve. Mix with all the remaining compote ingredients, including the raspberries. Divide this mixture between four ovenproof dessert bowls (12 fl oz/350 ml capacity).

3. Make up the soufflé topping as described in steps 2–4 on page 132, using Cointreau in place of the rum. Dollop it on top of the fruit mixture.

4. Bake in the oven for 15–20 minutes, until the topping has puffed up, and the compote is bubbling. Let cool for 5–10 minutes on a rack before serving. (It also tastes wonderful when thoroughly cooled.)

Cherry Cream

MAKES ½ PINT (300 ml)

LUMPS of cherry and bits of dark chocolate enrich creamy ricotta; vanilla and Cointreau perfume it. Serve in goblets as a kind of mousse, or use to top sliced peaches or fresh berries.

---

7 oz (200 g) carton quark
9 oz (250 g) carton ricotta
1–2 tablespoons morello cherry conserve
1 teaspoon natural vanilla extract

1 teaspoon Cointreau (optional)
½ oz (15 g) high-cocoa-solid dark
*   chocolate, grated*

Put all the ingredients in a food processor, and process until fluffy and very well mixed.

Chocolate-Dipped Apricots

TO END the collection, an elegant little sweetmeat to nibble with coffee. The chocolate cools to a brittle shell; the apricots remain chewy and juicy – a great contrast!

1. Melt some best-quality dark chocolate (at least 70 per cent cocoa solids). Dip ready-to-eat dried apricots in the melted chocolate, so they are half coated. Let cool on waxed or greaseproof paper.

2. Store in individual paper cases in an airtight tin in the fridge.

Index

Mail Order Guide

The following will all supply their goods by mail order. Contact them by phone or fax for details.

Low fat unsweetened cocoa powder
Excellent quality high cocoa solids
   dark chocolate

Terence Fisher
Chocolate Wholesaler
The Chestnuts
Earl Soham
Woodbridge
Suffolk
IP13 7RN

Tel: 01728 685529
Fax: 01728 685843

Cookware
Pure natural vanilla extract
Pure natural lemon and almond extracts

Lakeland Plastics
Alexandra Buildings
Winderemere
Cumbria
LA23 1BQ

Pure natural vanilla extract
Made in America
Hathaway Retail Park
Chippenham
SN15 1JG

Tel: 01249 447558
Fax: 01249 446142